THE WIT
OF GOLF

THE WIT OF GOLF

Compiled by Barry Johnston

Illustrated by John Ireland

HODDER &
STOUGHTON

First published in Great Britain in 2010 by Hodder & Stoughton
An Hachette UK company

1

Copyright © Barry Johnston 2010 in the arrangement
Extracts © individual copyright holders
Illustrations © John Ireland 2010

A CIP catalogue record for this title is available from the British Library.

ISBN 978 0 340 91935 4

Typeset in Sabon by Hewer Text UK Ltd, Edinburgh
Printed and bound by CPI Mackays, Chatham ME5 8TD

Hodder & Stoughton policy is to use papers that are natural, renew-
able and recyclable products and made from wood grown in sustainable
forests. The logging and manufacturing processes are expected to conform to
the environmental regulations of the country of origin.

Hodder & Stoughton Ltd
338 Euston Road
London NW1 3BH

www.hodder.co.uk

To Boo, Fuzzy, Golden Bear, Great White Shark,
Merry Mex and Tiger.

CONTENTS

FOREWORD

Golf, more than any other sport, has the ability to inspire both joy and despair in equal measure. As Sir Winston Churchill once put it, 'Golf is a game in which you try to put a small ball in a small hole with implements singularly unsuited to the purpose!'

For some players golf is almost a religion, a way of life they could not imagine giving up. The comedian Bob Hope was so hooked on the game that he said, 'Golf is my profession. I tell jokes to pay my green fees!' For others the game is simply a good excuse to meet up with their friends every weekend. There are even one or two misguided persons who fail to see the point of golf at all. Mark Twain famously described golf as 'a good walk spoiled' and Sir Michael Parkinson was the founder-member and president of the Anti-Golf Society before he saw the error of his ways. He was converted to the game, he says, because 'even when the sun goes behind a cloud, there is always a laugh to be had.'

For whenever two golfers are gathered together, you can be sure there will be funny stories. In compiling this book, I have read countless autobiographies and memoirs and consulted dozens of websites. Here are the very best anecdotes, as told by some of our greatest British golfers – Nick Faldo, Tony Jacklin, Sandy Lyle, Sam Torrance and Ian Woosnam. There are also unforgettable broadcasting gaffes and memories from two of our best-loved television commentators, Peter Alliss and Alex Hay.

The American journalist Robert Sommers has put together an excellent collection called *Golf Anecdotes* and I have been able to include several of his classic tales, from the golden era of Bobby Jones and Walter Hagen to the 'Big Three' of the 1960s – Arnold Palmer, Jack Nicklaus and Gary Player. Another great source of stories is the pro-celebrity golf circuit. Many showbusiness personalities have become extremely accomplished players and we have humorous contributions from stars such as Ronnie Corbett, Bruce Forsyth, Tom O'Connor and Michael Parkinson. The comedian and broadcaster Tim Brooke-Taylor adds his own witty observations with 'The Golfer's Hall of Fame' and 'The Golfing Book of Records'.

Some of the best sports journalism has been written about golf and I have selected some amusing pieces by Peter Dobereiner and Martin Johnson, as well as extracts from two more recent golf books, *Quiet Please* by Lawrence Donegan and *Bring Me the Head of Sergio Garcia!* by Tom Cox. There has also been a long tradition of golf stories in fiction, as demonstrated here with some hilarious examples by Patrick Campbell, Michael Green and the incomparable P.G. Wodehouse, and a delightful poem by John Betjeman.

Golf is a game full of highs and lows, which is why it can produce such great humour. I hope you enjoy reading this collection as much as I have enjoyed compiling it. As Ian Poulter said during the 2009 Open, after finally making a birdie on the 17th hole of his second round, 'You can only laugh!'

Barry Johnston
2010

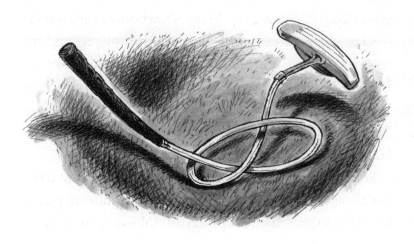

THE PRACTICE GROUND

Barry Johnston:

In an interview with *Golf Digest* magazine in 2002, Gary Player revealed the origin of his most famous quote. Many years earlier he was practising in a bunker in Texas when a local 'good old boy' wearing a large cowboy hat stopped to watch him. Player's first shot went straight in the hole. The Texan said, 'You got fifty bucks if you knock the next one in.' Player holed that shot, too. Still unconvinced, the man challenged him again, 'You got one hundred bucks if you hole the next one.'

The next three balls in a row all went in. As he peeled off the dollar bills, the Texan declared, 'Boy, I've never seen anyone so lucky in my life.'

Player shot back, 'Well, the harder I practise, the luckier I get!'

Nick Faldo:

Preparing for a trip to Switzerland, I needed to test a few three-woods and so I grabbed six clubs and whizzed off to Wentworth late one evening to decide which one suited me best. I painstakingly marked all the balls (about a dozen for each club) and put a corresponding mark on the six three-woods so that I could monitor distance and accuracy. I had whacked all 72 balls when I saw a little head pop up through the bushes about 150 yards away. I packed my clubs away in the car and set off down the fairway to see which club had performed the best but, as a big favour to me, my watcher had scooped all 72 balls into a neat pyramid.

He beamed, 'I thought I'd help!'

Barry Johnston:

Lee Trevino began his golfing career as a caddie at the Dallas Athletic Club in Texas, earning just $30 a week. Behind the caddie shed there were three short holes and after work the young Trevino would practise his golf every day, hitting more than three hundred balls in a session. He says, 'There is no such thing as natural touch. Touch is something you create by hitting millions of golf balls.'

The wisecracking Mexican-American, known as 'The Merry Mex' as well as 'Super Mex', went on to win six

majors between 1968 and 1984, including consecutive Open Championships, although he was entirely self-taught.

He once joked, 'I've never had a coach in my life. When I find one who can beat me, then I'll listen!'

Tom Cox: *Bring Me the Head of Sergio Garcia!*

I was playing the worst golf of my life and I decided that there were two main causes for my devastating play. One was the Panicked Squid. The other was the Evil Brain Worm. I refrained from explaining this theory to those closest to me, for fear of prompting them to sneak out of the room to make some discreet enquiries with mental-health charities. Instead, I examined the evidence, and tried to decide which of these two foes I needed to conquer first.

The Evil Brain Worm – formerly known as the Maggot,

before it grew to unmanageable size – represented the psychological side of my game. Like all golfers, I had always had it. It lived in that fertile part of my brain that responds to the command 'Don't think of a hippopotamus!' by thinking of a hippopotamus. It had popped up every now and then in the past, when I had been compiling a good score and trying not to hit the ball into a lake, and done its duty by reminding me that there was a lake in the vicinity. On the whole, I had been able to ignore it and control it. More recently, though, I'd got interested in it, and if there was one thing the Evil Brain Worm thrived on, it was attention.

'What,' the Evil Brain Worm would ask, 'if you lined up this simple short putt perfectly, attempted to make the absolutely perfect stroke, but then I shouted "Miss it!" just as you took the putter back? Would you miss it? And, if you did, wouldn't it be weird, that I had all that power?'

But the Evil Brain Worm was not always so loquacious. Sometimes it would just have to make a noise – 'Boo!' perhaps, or 'Flunt!', or 'Unkulspagger!' – at the exact moment when I was starting my backswing, in order to do its damage. It didn't have to form proper sentences to make its intentions lucid. It really was a wriggly, insidious bastard. I suppose, though, if it hadn't been, it wouldn't have been a very effective Evil Brain Worm.

The Panicked Squid, which represented the physical

side of my golfing make-up, might have been uncharitably viewed as a bigger, more hideous and tentacled version of the Evil Brain Worm. But I knew it wasn't anywhere near as malevolent. It meant well, and it wasn't its fault if it got confused. It was simply what happened when an instruction like 'Keep your swing nice and loose' transformed, in the heat of tournament play, into 'Make your swing a flailing mêlée of appendages.' In truth, it was probably controlled by the Evil Brain Worm, and served as its writhing, outward manifestation.

Bearing in mind that Darth Vader was nowhere near as much of a nasty piece of work as the Emperor in the *Star Wars* trilogy, there seemed to be only one way to go here, and that was straight to the source, cutting out the middleman. Or, in this case, the middle-squid.

I had been intending to do some work with a sports psychologist all year and I had an exploratory conversation with a member of the mind-coaching industry, Peter Crone. He unnerved me slightly.

'Don't take this the wrong way,' he told me over the phone, 'but from what you've been saying so far I gather you're a very sensitive person.'

This seemed a remarkably astute observation, given that we had only been speaking for three minutes at that point!

Michael Parkinson:

Playing a game with friends the other day, I noticed my partner had a card clipped to his bag on which he had listed the main points he had to remember before he swung the club. There were twenty headings. The pilot of a jumbo jet has less to worry about before he safely delivers four hundred passengers and several tons of metal on to the tarmac.

This set me thinking of the kind of information I had absorbed about the game from various sources over the years, and what I had been programmed to remember every time I picked up a golf club.

First of all, the grip. I was told not to grip the club too fiercely, to imagine it was a dove in my hands and I was throttling it but not taking its head off. Then the hands should not be too far from the body. Imagine if you are a man, you are having a pee and that is where the hands should be. All important is body posture over the ball. Ideally, I was to imagine that I was perched on a bar stool while leaning over a fence.

Remember the take-away must be smooth and flowing. Imagine you have a bucket of water in your hands. If you can take it back from the address without spilling any, that is what is required.

Alternatively, you can imagine yourself to be a windmill, or a particularly interesting image is to picture

yourself with your head through a pane of glass and able to swing the club without breaking anything.

I've never been able to understand that one, but the advice remains stuck to my brain like grease on a plate. At the top of the backswing with the club-head pointing at the target, don't forget that the back leg should be rigid as if encased in plaster. Or that's what I was told.

I was also advised that to facilitate the proper action in the downswing I must transfer the weight from the leg in the plaster cast to the leg without one. It would help, or so they said, if I imagined pulling a rope with a bell on it.

So what we have so far is a man sitting on a bar stool leaning over a fence while taking a leak, with his head stuck through a pane of glass and one leg in plaster.

That's only the half of it and I still haven't hit the ball!

Tim Brooke-Taylor:
RUPERT BROOKE

Struck the church clock at ten to three
And is my golf ball on the tee
And will the flag appear to move
Just as I swing with arms held smooth

And causing me one shoulder raise
And catch the ball a passing graze

And cuff it lightly o'er the top
That sends it in a five-foot hop

And would my shoulder ligaments tear
And cause me to scream and swear
And kick my foot and stub my toe
And make it start to throb and glow

And would I say you little tit
And boot it forward in a fit
And when my partner did protest
Would I say shut your gob you pest

And would I vengefully destroy
All the equipment at my employ
The marker box, the bench, the tee
And go upon a vengeful spree

And when I'd fully spent my ire
Would I calm down and say 'Right, squire
That is enough of practising
Now let's get on with the real thing!'

Patrick Campbell:

When it comes to having golf lessons there are two strict rules to be observed.

(1) Select a professional who really knows what he's talking about. There are several of them around.

(2) Keep all well-meaning friends – and in particular well-meaning fathers – away from the initiation ceremony, or you won't get a crack at it yourself.

I should like to illustrate what happens, if these two rules are ignored, by Case History Number One – Peter, a lightweight lad of sixteen, whose natural talents lie more in the direction of painting. Peter's golf-playing father, resisted all the way by Peter's mother, wants him to take up golf because it's more manly than messing about with Art.

Father is there on the practice ground for Peter's first lesson.

Not wishing to interfere with the lad's concentration, he parks the new, dark-green Rolls with the white-walled tyres under a nearby tree, to keep the sun off it, and sits unobtrusively at the wheel, smoking a straight-grained pipe.

Unfortunately, they haven't been able to get hold of the professional himself, so the first lesson is being given by the assistant, a lanky and not entirely competent youth called Dick.

By the look of him Dick estimates that Peter has sufficient physical co-ordination to give him a chance, by exerting it to the full, of turning himself into a fair hand at draughts.

Dick begins to demonstrate the Vardon Grip, wishing that the pupil's old man were farther away – in some place like the bar in the clubhouse or, preferably, Bermuda.

Ten minutes later Peter is locked in the state of rigor mortis natural to his first experience of the Vardon Grip.

'That's nice,' says Dick. 'Just try a swing. We'll see how it goes.'

With infinite care, it's all he can do to move – Peter slowly lifts the stick into the air until it achieves a semi-vertical position, slowly brings it down again and raises it into a similar position on the other side. At the lowest point of the arc the club-head passes three inches above the ground.

As always, with a new pupil, Dick is stunned by the sheer paralytic hopelessness of it. It beats him, completely, why the ass doesn't just swish it back, shift his weight into it and flash the club-head through. He's wondering, as ever, where to begin on this mess when a loud, cheerful voice comes from the Rolls.

'Rather picking it up with the wrists, there, Pete, old chap. You want the club, left hand and left arm moving back all in the one piece.'

Dick clenches his teeth. It's started. 'Just try another swing,' he tells his pupil. 'Take the club-head back a bit closer to the ground.'

Five minutes later Peter, having sensibly made his own furtive easement of the impossible rigours of the Vardon Grip, manages after three wispy air-shots to knock one twenty yards along the ground with a seven-iron.

'That's nice,' says Dick. 'That's coming.' He remembers who, and what, pays the rent. 'That right elbow's wandering a bit, though,' he says. 'If you cock up that elbow you're going to be outside the line going back. The right elbow,' says Dick, 'should be located close to the body until just after the moment of impact, providing a fulcrum to which the inside-out plane of the down swing can be anchored. You may find it helpful to put a handkerchief . . .'

'I don't want to butt in, but I think he'd find it easier to concentrate on a firm left arm,' says Peter's father, who's strolled over from the Rolls. 'Give me that stick a sec, Pete,' says Peter's father. 'Of course,' he tells Dick, 'I can't quite get as far back as you young chaps – anno domini, you know – but surely if you take the club and the left hand and arm back in the one piece . . .'

Peter's father makes the preliminary movement. He has a better idea. 'Chuck a ball down there,' he says. 'I'll show you what I mean.'

The first one nearly cuts the head off a man trying to hole a match-saver on the 18th, away to the left. 'That's all that damn nonsense about anchoring the right elbow,' says Peter's father cheerfully. 'You see what happens?' he tells his son.

After the next one the four men on the 18th become convinced that a personal attack is being made upon them, for reasons beyond their imagining. They come together in a belligerent group, glaring across at their attacker on the practice ground.

Peter's father is oblivious to them. With a stiffer left arm than he's ever used before he's sliced three into the wood, in the opposite direction, and is now putting the whole thing down to a fault in his stance, or a premature transference of weight after the initial movement of the down swing.

'Watch this one,' he tells Dick roughly. 'I may be getting the left hip out of the way too late.'

Peter, the novice, the learner, stands there with a great weight on his soul. He'd thought, the first time he picked one up, that it wasn't going to be very easy with these long, heavy, narrow-headed sticks to hit such a small ball very far – or even at all – but never in his lowest moment had he guessed that the process was going to be governed by so many anatomical impossibilities.

Peter's first and almost certainly last lesson concludes with Peter sitting on the grass picking daisies in lacklustre fashion, while Dick tries to think of something – anything – that will stop Peter's father losing yet another of Dick's practice balls in the wood!

Barry Johnston:

Princess Liliane of Belgium, the second wife of Leopold III, was a very keen golfer and she once asked John Jacobs for advice on how to improve her game. Jacobs watched the princess hit a few practice balls and he concluded that her grip was too strong.

'You may be a princess,' Jacobs informed her, 'but if you hold the club like that, you will always be a hooker!'

Nick Faldo:

My various rebuilds, painful as they may have been, were not without their lighter moments and several amusing incidents occurred during the countless practice sessions at Wentworth.

'Do you mind if I watch?' came a voice once from over my shoulder as I tipped out the balls. I far prefer working in private but, having been brought up to be polite, I replied, 'Yeah, that's fine,' whereupon I proceeded to hit four five-irons slap-bang down the middle. No exaggeration, the four balls finished up on all four corners of a square yard. Flexing my muscles, I thought 'Well, that's all right.' I took a practice swing, at which point I heard, 'Excuse me, but did you know your practice swing is nothing like your real swing?'

The next six balls flew left, right, left, right, left, right, all over the place, at which point I packed up and went home!

CADDIES

Barry Johnston:

Jerry 'Hobo' Osborn has been a caddie on the Senior PGA Tour (now the Champions Tour) in the USA for more than twenty years and in that time he has worked for most of the senior players. After being on the receiving end of years of complaints, insults and general abuse on the golf course, Jerry has developed his own careworn philosophy of the game.

He says, 'Players make mistakes. Caddies make blunders!'

Nick Faldo:

Dave McNeilly is an Ulsterman with more than a touch of blarney. I first met Dave, a total eccentric in the nicest possible way, in America in the early 1980s. Although

16

totally different in personality, we seemed to hit it off and I made arrangements to engage him full-time on my return to England for the Dunlop Masters at Lindrick.

'Oh, do you do yardages?' I asked, almost as an after-thought, when I spoke to him on the phone.

'Yes, indeed I do.'

'Do you have a wheel?' I continued, referring to the device caddies use for measuring exact distances.

'. . . eh, no, I use public transport.'

Dave, honest soul that he is, was forever getting hold of the wrong end of the stick.

'We'll need to get a video,' I informed him on the practice ground one morning while working on my swing.

'Oh, yeah,' he agreed enthusiastically. 'Have you seen *Jaws 2*?'

Sandy Lyle:

As likeable as he is, in the caddie shed Seve Ballesteros was not renowned as the easiest man to work with, and the popular joke was that he worked his way through more caddies than Joan Collins did husbands.

One yarn centred around an incident at the Spanish Open one year when Seve turned to his then favourite, Martin Gray, and asked for a piece of fruit.

'Too bitter,' complained Seve, tasting the proffered orange.

'Too brown,' he bemoaned, rejecting a banana.

'Too soft,' he grimaced, handing back an apple.

'Listen, Seve,' Gray finally snapped. 'I'm a caddie, not a greengrocer!'

Ian Woosnam:

Most professional golfers treat their caddies like friends. Some treat them like employees. A few treat them like children. Through fourteen years together, Wobbly was more like a brother to me.

This lanky, permed, curly-haired Yorkshireman was christened Philip Morbey, but most people in the golfing world know him as 'Wobbly'. In fact, that's his full name. Usually, he's just 'Wobs'.

He apparently earned this nickname because of the way he walks, but there was nothing wobbly about his performance at my side, carrying the bag. From 1987 until 2001, he was a rock of knowledge, commitment and support. In so many ways, Wobbly was a massive part of my success in golf.

Before I hired Wobbly, I asked around about him, and David Jagger was kind enough to tell me exactly how this lively, young character had got started as a caddie on the Tour.

Wobbly was just seventeen at the time, earning a living by stocking shelves at his local supermarket, but he had set his heart on being a caddie. One afternoon, he plucked up the courage to approach 'Jags' who happened to be the touring professional attached to his local golf club in Selby, East Yorkshire.

'So you want to be a caddie on the professional Tour?'

'Yes, Mr Jagger,' Wobbly replied.

'All right,' Jags replied. 'Well, there is a strict procedure for caddies. First, you have to take a test; and if you do well, you get a pass; and you need that pass before you can caddie on Tour.'

'I see.'

'So, if you want, you can take your test at eight o'clock tomorrow. Can you be here?'

'Of course I can.'

Wobbly was excited and nervous when he arrived at the club the following morning. Jags appeared and asked him to fetch his bag of clubs from the boot of his car. As soon as he lifted the bag on his shoulder, Wobbly thought it seemed strangely heavy. In fact, it was unbelievably heavy, but he didn't say anything because he wanted to pass his test and he was desperate to make a good impression.

By the time he reached the 5th green, Wobbly was clearly breathing hard. He was sweating at the 9th tee and, approaching the 18th, he was scarcely able to walk. Jags had led him all over the course, up and down hills, through trees and bunkers, but Wobbly shouldered his burden and followed.

'Well done, Wobbly,' said Jags at the end of the round, as the young caddie stood exhausted in the car park. 'You have done very well. I will send a full report to the PGA and, hopefully, they will agree to issue you with a pass. You will then have to wait until it arrives in the post.'

'OK, Mr Jagger. Thank you very much, Mr Jagger.'

As soon as Wobbly was out of sight, Jags took the clubs out of his bag and carefully removed the three bricks he had placed at the bottom of the bag earlier that morning!

Jags took Wobbly as his caddie on Tour soon afterwards, but almost a year passed and Wobbly was still anxiously checking his post, waiting for his caddie pass to arrive from the PGA. Only then, one night in the pub, with people laughing so hard they were falling off chairs, did Jags have the heart to tell Wobbly that, in fact, the whole test had been a joke and there was no such thing as a caddie's pass.

Even then, Wobbly looked more disappointed than angry!

Barry Johnston:

In the 1960 US Open at Cherry Hills, in Denver, Colorado, Dow Finsterwald finished tied-third, behind Arnold Palmer and Jack Nicklaus. He might even have won the championship if he had listened more to his caddie.

At one point his caddie was heard to complain, 'Why ask me? You've asked me two times already and paid no attention to what I said. Pick your own club!'

Peter Dobereiner:

No golfer ever fought and won a more savage battle with his turbulent nature than Neil Coles. I treasure many memories of Coles and his regular caddie, Arthur Maidment, who was known universally in British golf as 'Chingy'. At Sunningdale they had one of their regular disagreements over clubbing and this altercation resulted in the ludicrous spectacle of Coles tugging furiously at the head of his four-wood while Chingy tenaciously clung to the grip and tried to pull the offending club from his master. They looked for all the world like two starlings engaged in a tug o' war with a worm.

Finally Coles gained possession of the club, brute strength prevailing over the ageing Chingy, and he hit a glorious shot from deep heather to four feet from the flag. He glared at Chingy with an expression compounded of triumph and contempt as he slammed the club back into the bag.

Chingy, never lacking in spirit and determined to have the last word, replied fiercely: 'You would have been closer with the three-iron!'

Nick Faldo:

It was at the 1976 British Open Championship at Royal Birkdale that I had my first argument with that most curious of breeds, the old-school, battle-hardened, seen-it-all caddie. To Paddy, the crazy Irishman of Royal Birkdale, Nick Faldo was an intrusive nuisance to be tolerated for the one and only reason that Paddy was being paid to do so.

One of Paddy's many idiosyncrasies was to don shoes he found lying about the locker room, no matter to whom they belonged and even if they were four sizes too big. He would totter to the first tee looking like Coco the Clown.

After the third round on the Saturday night, rather than taking my clubs into the clubhouse, he left my bag leaning against an outside wall, whereupon Birkdale was hit by an almighty thunderstorm and torrential rain. When I came out, the water was pouring out of the top of my bag and after a real set-to in the car park, I sacked Paddy on the spot. It was only after he disappeared round the corner into an unknown future that I realised he had made off in a pair of my best shoes!

Barry Johnston:

Lee Trevino won six majors but he started out as a caddie, so he speaks from experience when he says: 'Nobody but you and your caddie care what you do out there, and if your caddie is betting against you, he doesn't care, either!'

Ian Woosnam:

Bernhard Langer is only six months older than me, but he turned professional at the age of eighteen and made his first appearance on Tour in 1971. Incredibly, he finished in the top five on the European Order of Merit in twelve of the fifteen years between 1981 and 1995, emerging as a remarkably consistent, dedicated player. There are no sides to Bernhard at all: he works hard, and he remains constant, unchanged and unfailingly friendly.

Famous for using a compass to check the direction of the wind during practice rounds, his preparation is meticulous to the point of being scientific. He notes every yardage. There is a story that Bernhard once asked his caddie for the distance from a sprinkler head in the fairway to the front of the green.

'It's 114 yards,' Pete Coleman, his long-time caddie, replied.

'Is that from the front or the back of the sprinkler head?'

Barry Johnston:

This story is told about several professional golfers, all of whom deny that it has anything to do with them! Apparently, one day a very well-known golfer noticed that his caddie was wearing a shoe with a loose sole. It made a flapping noise when he walked. The golfer pointed this out to his caddie and told him he needed to buy a new pair of trainers.

'I know, guv,' said the bag-carrier, looking rather embarrassed, 'but I haven't got enough money.'

'Don't worry,' said his boss, kindly, 'I'll help you.'

The golfer reached into his trouser pocket and pulled out a huge wad of notes held together by a thick rubber band. His caddie looked on in amazement at this unexpected generosity. Then the golfer peeled off the rubber band and handed it to his caddie.

'Here,' he said, 'try that!'

Nick Faldo:

A popular caddie was 'The Prof'. Whenever we played in the Benson & Hedges at York, he would find a cheap room in one of the university halls of residence. He was idly minding his own business over a pint or five in the uni bar one evening when a genteel, professional voice at his side enquired, 'I say, old chap, what are you reading?'

'Greens,' came the reply.

Sandy Lyle:

In the 1983 Madrid Open I entered the final round in second place, two shots in arrears of Gordon J. Brand. As the weather deteriorated, play was suspended – in all, the final 'afternoon' lasted the best part of eight hours – and my caddie, Dave Musgrove, as only he could, disappeared to enjoy a four-course lunch, including roast lamb and mint sauce, reappearing with a huge self-satisfied grin on his face.

Replete or not, Dave was always sound in the advice he gave. Gordon, however, wasn't so lucky. His caddie at the time was a retired teacher, popularly known as 'Snitch' because of his curious nasal tones. On the par-three 17th, 193 yards into a stiff wind, and with me holding a slender one-shot lead, Gordon was uncertain about the right club to select and wisely asked Snitch his opinion.

Perhaps Snitch was feeling miffed that he didn't follow Mussie for a grand nosh-up when he had the opportunity. 'Take what you like, Gordon,' came the reply, 'they're all in there!'

Mussie bent double with his hand covering his mouth to stifle his laughter while I studiously surveyed the surrounding countryside. After scratching his head in puzzlement, Gordon eventually settled for a four-iron, the ball flew the green for a bogey and I won the tournament by two strokes!

Nick Faldo:

'Jungle Jim' used to be a well-known caddie on the European circuit, partly because of his liberal use of the 'F' word but mostly because he was the oddest-looking bugger ever to bestride a fairway. He had no teeth, and was rumoured to sleep rough in the bushes, and generally acquired a reputation as the wild man of the caddies' hut.

On one occasion, I was partnering a young rookie who had made the mistake of employing the battle-hardened Jungle Jim and the unnerved kid opened his round with five straight snap-hooks.

Jim's next comment didn't help. 'What did you have for effing breakfast? Effing bananas?'

Michael Parkinson:

A lifetime spent observing the human race at its most absurd has given most caddies a deft line in dry humour. A friend of mine, a notoriously bad-tempered player, was coming down the homeward straight after a round that had sorely tried his self-control. Playing his approach shot for the final green he landed deep in a bunker. At this he went berserk and, after trying to break his club over his knee (a singularly futile and painful pastime), he hurled the wretched iron far into a clump of dense bracken.

There was a silence, broken only by the sound of my friend's heavy breathing and the voice of his caddie who whispered into his left earhole, 'If I were you, sir, I'd take the optional club!'

Peter Dobereiner:

In many cases the caddie performs a valuable passive role as a convenient scapegoat. When a player mishits a shot it is excellent therapy for him to be able to turn on the caddie and berate him roundly for some imaginary malfeasance, misfeasance or nonfeasance. That is accepted by the caddies as all part of the job although, occasionally, this function of being used as a receptacle for vented spleen becomes too much to bear.

28

On one memorable occasion at Wentworth the Professor laid down Ken Brown's bag and gave the golfer a stern lecture on the unprofessional practice of throwing in the towel.

'The one thing I cannot stand,' said the Professor, 'is a quitter.'

Whereupon he quit and walked back to the clubhouse!

Barry Johnston:

Gary Player took his regular caddie, Alfred 'Rabbit' Dyer, with him to the 1974 Open Championship at Royal Lytham and St Annes. It was the first time a black man had ever caddied in the championship. Before the tournament, Player warned Dyer, 'Make sure you wear your badge here, Rabbit. They're very strict, just like at Augusta or the US Open.'

Dyer looked at the sea of white faces around him and simply shrugged. He said, 'Don't worry about me, boss. I stick out here like a fly in buttermilk!'

Nick Faldo:

Over in America, Fulton Allem was enduring a miserable round at Hilton Head, dropping shots all over the place and missing a series of short putts. After three-putting the 13th, Fulton snapped the head off his putter and stormed off to the 14th tee where he proceeded to smash the marker before looking round frantically and demanding, 'What else can I break?'

'How about par,' muttered his bag-carrier darkly.

Tim Brooke-Taylor:
THE GOLFING BOOK OF RECORDS

Undoubtedly the dubious honour of 'The Rudest Caddie' goes to Sagemore Tuffit, a West Country caddie who was known to have 'the foulest tongue in all of Somerset'. Even before a ball had been played he would have rudely denounced the player, his family and his family's family in a torrent of slanderous abuse. And all this after simply being asked what club the hole played. He would then go on to accuse the player's wife of being a black Jezebel, and the player himself of being the product of wedlock between a donkey and a cabbage. Throughout the round, Sagemore would continue his vitriolic diatribe, swearing and cursing and accusing the player of every sin under the sun.

After a while it became quite fashionable to be partnered on your round by Sagemore, and he drew a quite enviable following as players flocked to become the butt of his fiery tongue. Indeed, such was the demand for his services that some players would refuse to turn out unless they had Sagemore at their side, heaping scorn on their game and their private lives.

At last, as the pressure began to tell, Sagemore started to run out of things to say and would simply spend the entire round blowing raspberries whenever his player was playing, and when addressed for any reason would simply resort to screaming 'pink blancmange' at the top of his voice before attacking the nearest player with an ice-pick.

He eventually retired from the world of golf and was last heard of working for British Gas!

CLUB GOLF

Peter Alliss:

For Jackie and me, our time at Moor Allerton Golf Club, on the north side of Leeds, was fulfilling and educational and gave us fascinating insights into the Jewish way of life. We had been warmly welcomed and made some wonderful friends. In the early days I had long conversations with a dear old boy called Doddy Aber who insisted on calling me 'Mr Alliss'. He regaled me with tales of the Jewish culture.

I liked Moor Allerton because it had a caring ethos. They looked after their old folk. Many of them observed the Friday night customs, the family circle. The club closed early on a Friday so as not to offend those who still maintained the standards of yesterday. They were not great drinkers but they had a beautiful bar at the club.

Perhaps most of all I loved their sense of humour: General Moshe Dyan was asked how he had managed to win the Six Day War – it was over in a flash. 'Well,' he said, 'I lined up all the doctors on the left, all the lawyers on the right and all the accountants in the middle, then I stood on a hill and shouted "Charge" and, boy, do those guys know how to charge!'

And one must not forget the Jewish lament: if Moses had turned right instead of left when he crossed the Red Sea, we'd have had all the oil and the Arabs would have had the oranges!

Michael Parkinson:

In the West Indies beach cricket is not an alternative to the real thing; it is a training ground for the international arena. That explains why I once played several games out there and can honestly say I never saw a ball that was bowled at me.

It was this traumatic experience as much as anything that led me into golf's seductive embrace. I had retired hurt from my latest (and last) game of beach cricket and was attempting to get my bruises sunburned when the wife suggested I spend the sunlit days in pursuit of a less dangerous ambition.

I found a partner at the local golf club and embarked on my new venture. It had looked such a simple game I couldn't understand why I was so inept at it.

Nor did it help that my partner, a man well into his seventies who looked as if he might need a walking frame, knocked the ball about with easy nonchalance. He was polite and solicitous about my plight, until at the 10th hole I drove my ball into a snake-infested jungle and said, 'Who on earth built this bloody golf course?'

'As a matter of fact,' he said, 'I did!'

Alex Hay:

~~Jimmy Simpson~~ was a scratch player at Hartsbourne Country Club. Through his aggressive attitude and immense strength – he was almost as broad as he was tall – he had got to scratch in a very short time and was fanatical about the game. Rain, hail and, of course, snow, he played golf, much of it in the company of good professional players.

Years before, a friend had taken him to Hartsbourne and introduced him to Pat Keene, who was a well-known club professional, though rather a shrewd businessman. The bug got Jimmy, who, at that time, was a very successful car dealer, so he made an appointment to buy equipment from Pat. Arriving in the Hartsbourne Professional's Shop, Jimmy pulled from his pocket one of those wads of money that would choke a proverbial horse.

'I don't care what it costs,' he said, laying the massive bundle down on top of the counter. 'I want only the best!'

Pat Keene had a severe stammer, which tended to worsen as he got excited and now he was excited: this for him could be the sale of the century, a customer with so much money and no idea what he was buying. A golden opportunity to get rid of some dead stock if ever there was one. Soon Pat had a huge and hugely expensive leather bag filled with woods, irons, wedges and a putter. The pockets were filled with waterproofs, gloves and balls. Expensive leather covers were fitted to the clubs and the best veldtschoen shoes to Jimmy.

'Th-th-th-there you are, Sir.' Pat's excitement was almost overcoming him. 'Th-th-th-that'll be th-th-th-three hundred and fi-fi-fi-fifty p-p-p-pounds.' A vast sum in those days.

Jimmy picked up the wad and calmly counted out seventy of those large £5 notes, saying nothing until he completed. Then he turned to face Pat and, heaving his huge shoulders to their full width, he looked the beaming professional straight in the eyes.

'It is my intention to become not just a good golfer, but an extremely good golfer. When I do, if I find out that these are not the best clubs, then I shall bring them back to this shop and tie them around your effing neck!'

Pat hesitated, his hand frozen half-way to the money. Then he turned towards the racks of clubs and said, 'In th-th-th-that case, you'd better have this set!'

Barry Johnston:

Two old golfers were playing a friendly round at their club but on the 1st tee one of them hooked and the other one sliced, so they did not meet up again until they were on the green.

'How many?' asked the first man.

'Seven,' replied his friend.

'Ah, then I've two for it,' said the first man jubilantly, and he proceeded to putt up to the hole and knock in the next.

At the 2nd tee, history repeated itself. The two men went their separate ways and came together again on the green. The first man was about to speak when his friend quickly held up his hand.

'My turn,' he said. 'How many?'

Tom O'Connor:

I heard a good story (and I have no reason to believe it is not true) from a snooty Home Counties club, where a party of ladies were sitting out on the verandah, watching a male four-ball coming up the 18th. One of the players obviously was heading for a very good score that only needed something like a par or a bogey to break the course record. But he duffed his second shot into the heather and it was totally unplayable. Understandably, he came out with a four-letter mouthful in sheer frustration.

On hearing this, one of the ladies got up and stormed into the secretary's office. 'This is disgusting,' she complained. 'I am out on the patio with a group of other ladies and we shouldn't have to put up with such disgraceful language from some of these so-called gentlemen – something should be done about it.'

The committee met and took it very seriously.

After a long deliberation they decided the best way to prevent this embarrassment happening again was to ban ladies from the verandah!

Peter Alliss:

For many years Hugh Lewis was the major domo at the Altrincham Municipal, some seven or eight miles south of Manchester. It was a very busy club and of good quality, well cared for, considering the amount of golf played there. Two occasions come to mind, one when he looked out of the shop window to see a youngish man pushing a pram up the fairway, parking it gently by the side of the green, taking a putter, which lay across the chassis, putting out, then moving on to the next tee.

Hugh couldn't resist asking him what was going on and was told that his wife didn't like him to go out to play golf and the only way he could escape her clutches was to say he'd take the baby for a walk, which he did. He hoped it was all right, and he knew that he shouldn't wheel the pram on to the greens. Hugh sent him on his way, with a smile (and a prayer!).

On another occasion he caught a golfer picking up divots, examining them and then placing them in his golf bag. It turned out he'd just moved to the town and had a very small area of ground between his front gate and front door. He was collecting divots to create a small lawn, one about three foot by seven foot, and he hoped it was okay to take them, for he'd noticed divots didn't grow back very often!

Well, what do you say?

Michael Parkinson:

Bunkers have destroyed golfers, turned strong men into gibbering wrecks. They are the ultimate obstacles in life, the supreme test of character. I have played with men who have thrown all their clubs, followed by their bag and the trolley over the cliffs after spending too long in a bunker. Sometimes they had to be restrained from following their equipment onto the rocks below.

I have also played with men who, faced with similar disasters, were so incredibly brave and humorous it made you proud to be marking their card. One chap I played with took six shots to get out of the bunker at Gleneagles and then putted back into the same bunker. All he said was, 'What a nuisance.'

Therefore, when Michael Barratt struck his second shot on the 7th, a benign par-four, into the greenside bunker, he felt nothing but sympathy and best wishes flowing towards him from Laurie 'Lozza' Holloway and myself. He was sitting in the middle of the bunker on flat sand so we didn't anticipate too much drama. His first shot lifted the ball in the air, which is the general idea, but didn't move it forward so it plopped back to something like its original position.

'Oh dear,' said Michael.

'Hard luck,' we said. His second shot did exactly the same.

'Damn,' said Michael. We made reassuring sounds. His third shot moved the ball forwards but not up in the air. He was doing all the right things but not at the same time. 'What is going on?' he asked. It was a rhetorical question. At the fourth attempt, he drove the ball into the face of the bunker. The crisis was increasing all the time, as were the comic possibilities.

'How many have I had in the bunker?' asked Michael.

'Four,' we told him. He looked so forlorn we wanted to adopt him. His next shot hit the underside lip of the bunker and flew behind him.

'What am I doing wrong?' he asked. Lozza suggested he take more sand. I managed to refrain from observing that there wasn't much left in the bunker, most of it having been deposited on the green, which looked like Clacton beach.

Attempting to follow instructions and by now a desperate man, Michael took a lot of sand but no ball in his next attempt. As a consequence, the sand flew upwards and caught the prevailing wind, blew back in his face and covered his body. When the sandstorm died down he was so perfectly camouflaged we could barely see him.

It was at this point that I noticed Lozza had a handkerchief in his mouth and his shoulders were shaking. My eyes were watering with suppressed mirth and I wanted to go to the toilet. The dam broke when the sand-blasted figure in the bunker said, 'And what's so bloody funny?'

At least that's what we think he said. It came out as 'Anwassoblurryunny,' which is how a man speaks with a mouthful of sand.

The trouble with laughing uncontrollably is that from a distance it seems as if you might have been shot or are having a fit. The team coming up behind us told us later that they were gravely concerned to see two of us doubled up and holding our bellies as if being sick while the other member of the team – by this time Michael had seen the funny side of his predicament too – appeared to have collapsed in a writhing heap in the bunker.

In the end, Michael took seven shots to get out of the sand and scored an 11. Six holes later, on the short par-three, he hit another bunker.

'Here we go again!' he said.

P.G. Wodehouse: The Heart of a Goof

It has been well said that there are many kinds of golf, beginning at the top with the golf of professionals and the best amateurs and working down through the golf of ossified men to that of Scotch University professors. Until recently this last was looked upon as the lowest possible depth; but nowadays, with the growing popularity of summer hotels, we are able to add a brand still lower, the golf you find at places like Marvis Bay.

To Ferdinand Dibble, coming from a club where the standard of play was rather unusually high, Marvis Bay was a revelation, and for some days after his arrival there he went about dazed, like a man who cannot believe it is really true. To go out on the links at this summer resort was like entering a new world. The hotel was full of stout, middle-aged men, who, after a misspent youth devoted to making money, had taken to a game at which real proficiency can only be acquired by those who start playing in their cradles and keep their weight down. Out on the course each morning you could see representatives of every nightmare style that was ever invented.

There was the man who seemed to be attempting to deceive his ball and lull it into a false sense of security by looking away from it and then making a lightning slash in the apparent hope of catching it off its guard. There was the man who wielded his mid-iron like one killing snakes. There was the man who addressed his ball as if he were stroking a cat, the man who drove as if he were cracking a whip, the man who brooded over each shot like one whose heart is bowed down by bad news from home, and the man who scooped with his mashie as if he were ladling soup.

By the end of the first week Ferdinand Dibble was the acknowledged champion of the place. He had gone through the entire menagerie like a bullet through a cream puff!

Tom O'Connor:

Then there is the expert ball marker – you must have met him. Instead of marking behind the ball, he marks in front. Then, when replacing the ball, he puts it in front of the marker.

I watched one from close up one day and a member of our four said, 'Careful, pal. If you mark that ball once more, you'll be in the hole!'

There is fun even in adversity on a golf course. Witness the bloke whose ball flew into a lake, infuriating him so much that he stormed in after it, his head gradually disappearing under the water, leaving only a floating cap.

After an interminable wait, the other three saw a hand rise as if grasping Excalibur and flicker gently.

'He's drowning for sure,' says one.

'Not necessarily,' says his partner. 'He could be calling for a five-iron!'

Peter Alliss:

Whilst I was living at Moor Allerton Golf Club I received this letter in a very impressive envelope, with 'The Rescue Mission, Birmingham' printed boldly on the back. It read:

Dear Mr Alliss

Perhaps you've heard of me and my nationwide campaign in the cause of Temperance. Each year for the past fourteen, I have made a tour of Scotland and the north of England, including Manchester, Glasgow and your town of Leeds, where I have delivered a series of lectures on the Evils of Drink. On this tour I have been accompanied by a young friend and assist-ant, David Powell. David, a young man from a good family, with an excellent background, is a pathetic example of a life ruined by excessive indulgence in alcohol and, may I add, women of a loose nature!

David would appear with me at lectures and sit on the platform wheezing, just staring at the audience through bleary, bloodshot eyes, sweating profusely, picking his nose, sometimes passing wind and making obscene gestures, while I would point out that he was an example of what drinking can do to a person.

Unfortunately, last summer David died. A mutual friend has given me your name and I wonder if you would care to take David's place on the next Tour?

Yours, in faith,
Reverend Rupert R. Knight
Rescue Mission

Michael Parkinson:

The joy of golf is that even when the sun goes behind a cloud there is always a laugh to be had. I was playing once with my good friend Mr James Tarbuck whose fanaticism about the game I can only liken to my father's attitude towards cricket. He was standing over a putt on the last hole of a course in Surrey where a public footpath runs close to the green. There was money on the shot and at such a moment Mr Tarbuck is not to be messed with. He had carefully and painstakingly lined up and had drawn the putter back when a citizen approached.

'Excuse me,' he said. Mr Tarbuck looked up in disbelief.

'Can you tell me how to get to the cemetery?' he enquired.

'Try dying,' said Mr Tarbuck, quite affably!

CHAMPIONS

Barry Johnston:

Annika Sörenstam is the most successful female golfer of all time. Before she retired from competitive golf in 2008, she won ninety international tournaments as a professional, including ten majors. The cool Swede was famous for her absolute concentration on the golf course and was sometimes criticised for not interacting more with the fans. She acknowledged, 'I find it very hard because I'm focusing. I've got something to do. I want to keep my mind on that and not let it wander on other things.'

Off the course Annika was far more relaxed and she would often play practical jokes on the other players, especially during her early days. In 1990 she made her debut as a member of the Swedish team that took part in the Women's World Amateur Team Championship, also known as the Espirito Santo Trophy.

That year the championship was held at Russley Golf Club in Christchurch, in New Zealand, and before the event started, Annika went out to a local store and bought some itching powder. Back in the locker room she sprinkled the contents of the packet inside the uniform of Pia Nilsson, who was the head coach of the Sweden team.

During the opening ceremony the Swedish coach could not stand still. Pia Nilsson tried desperately to maintain her composure, but she was an exercise in perpetual motion, itching and scratching from top to bottom, as the Swedish team stifled their giggles behind her.

Afterwards Annika confessed to Nilsson what she had done, but recalling the incident a few years later, she admitted, 'It was a long ceremony and we had a lot of fun!'

Sandy Lyle:

During his major-title barren years of 1980–86, Jack Nicklaus would happily tell the following joke at his own expense:

'A guy goes into a bar with his dog and orders a beer. The barman switches channels on the TV and on comes the latest golf tournament. I make a birdie and the dog does a back-flip on the bar. On the next hole, I sink another putt for a birdie and the dog repeats his

back-flip. "Your dog must be a real Nicklaus fan," says the barman. "What does he do when Nicklaus wins a tournament?"

'To which the guy replies, "I don't know, he's only six years old!"'

Sam Torrance:

Golf has always been a gambling game, from the 50p a corner OAP four-ball on a Wednesday afternoon to the great money matches that were so prevalent in the United States in the 1930s, when wagers exceeded prize money.

There was the wonderful story when Raymond Floyd was snared into taking on the unknown Lee Trevino at Horizon Hills in El Paso in 1965, a tale told by betting expert and golf writer Jeremy Chapman.

'Have you heard of Lee Trevino?' Alvin Clarence Thomas, a financial backer, asked Floyd.

'No,' Floyd replied, knowing a match was in the offing, 'but I'll play anyone anywhere that I've never heard of.'

Lee Trevino, writing in his book *Super Mex*, described their first meeting: 'I'd never met Raymond, so when he drove up I got a cart and went out to pick up his golf bag. I carried his clubs into the locker room, put them in a locker, brushed his shoes, cleaned them and polished them. Raymond asked me, "Who am I supposed to play?" and I said, "Me." He looked at me and said, "You? What do you do?" So I told him, "I'm a combination of everything. I'm the cart man, the shoe man, the clubhouse man and pro."'

Trevino won the first two matches with 65s, Floyd the third to win some of his pride and money back. He departed muttering something about finding easier ways to make a living!

Barry Johnston:

Tiger Woods is renowned for his total dedication to golf. He has admitted, 'The only thing that means a lot to me is winning. If I have more wins than anybody else and win more majors than anybody else in the same year, then it's been a good year.' But he still retains a sense of humour. He says, 'If you can't laugh at yourself, then who can you laugh at?'

Tiger once commented, 'Hockey is a sport for white men. Basketball is a sport for black men. Golf is a sport for white men dressed like black pimps!'

Sandy Lyle:

Arnold Palmer won seven majors and remains the main reason why golf has become a multi-million-dollar entertainment industry. Long before the emergence of Seve Ballesteros, it was Palmer, with his dashing good looks, stevedore's physique and riverboat gambler's instinct, who attracted the first huge golf galleries the world over.

The public loved him so because they knew every time Palmer reached for a club it was show time! Playing in the Los Angeles Open in 1961, Palmer took a ruinous 13 on one hole when he refused his caddie's advice to lay up short on a par-five with victory seemingly certain. 'Take an iron,' pleaded his bag carrier. 'It's my reputation,' replied Arnie, taking a long draw on his cigarette. 'Give me the goddamn wood.' The ball flew into the water guarding the green and from there calamity followed calamity.

Asked to explain how he had run up thirteen shots, Palmer grinned and drawled, 'It was easy, I missed a twenty-foot putt for a twelve!'

Michael Parkinson:

Walter Hagen had some good advice for golfers. He said, 'Don't hurry. Don't worry. You're only here on a short visit, so don't forget to stop and smell the roses.' Not only did Mr Hagen practise what he preached, but he ordered that the words be inscribed on his coffin when he died.

I have always found Walter Hagen one of the most fascinating figures in sport. Between 1914 and 1929 he won the British Open four times, the US Open twice, and the American PGA Championship five times.

This is all the more remarkable when you consider it was achieved by a man who chain-smoked, drank a lot of whiskey and was never known to refuse a party. After winning the Canadian Open he wired ahead to his hotel: 'Fill one bathtub of champagne.'

On the last day of the PGA Championship, when Hagen was due to play Leo Diegel for what was then the highest prize in professional golf, he arrived at the course wearing a dinner jacket after a night on the town. He was seen by a fan who said: 'Do you know that Diegel has been in bed since ten o'clock last night?'

'He might have been in bed,' said Hagen, 'but he wasn't sleeping!'

He beat Diegel 5 and 3.

Sandy Lyle:

Although Billy Casper was victorious in just three majors, he won 51 tournaments on the US Tour, played in seven successful Ryder Cup teams, compiling 20 wins and seven halves from his 37 matches, and is regarded as one of the finest putters the game has ever known. As his fellow US Tour pro Chi Chi Rodriguez said of him, 'Billy was the greatest putter I ever saw. When golf balls left the factory they used to pray they would get putted by Billy Casper!'

Quiet, a devout Mormon and eminently likeable, Casper and his wife, Shirley, raised eleven children, six of whom they adopted from the Far East, which says a lot about him as a man. As a golfer, he has always been curiously underrated by the galleries but certainly not by his contemporaries.

'I felt sorry for Billy out there today,' said Gary Player during Casper's 1966 US Open victory at the Olympic

Club, San Francisco. 'He couldn't putt a lick – I saw him miss three thirty-footers!'

Barry Johnston:

Even though he is only five feet four inches tall, Ian Woosnam has always been able to drive a golf ball further than most of his contemporaries. After the diminutive Welshman beat Sandy Lyle in the final of the 1987 World Match Play Championship at Wentworth, Lyle declared, 'If he ever grows up, he'll hit the ball two thousand yards!'

Robert Sommers:

A young pro eager to improve his game asked Ben Hogan if he could give him any advice.

'Do you have any practice balls?' Hogan asked. Expecting to be led to the practice tee for a lesson, the young man assured him he did indeed have practice balls.

Hogan said, 'Then use them!'

Another young pro came to Hogan for help, saying he was having trouble with thirty- and forty-foot putts. Could Hogan offer him advice?

Hogan told him, 'Hit the ball closer to the hole!'

Sam Torrance:

'Look out for my young brother,' Manuel Ballesteros said to me, long before Seve came on Tour. 'He is going to be something special.' He certainly did not smell like anything special. My first ever encounter with the great man was at Dalmahoy, when he let rip with the most disgusting fart.

'That's diabolical,' I said, pretending to be offended.

Seve replied, 'I eat food, not flowers!'

Barry Johnston:

Walter Hagen had his own homespun philosophy about golf, and life in general. Most famously, he said, 'No one remembers who came second.' Hagen also declared, 'Give me a man with big hands, big feet and no brains and I'll make a golfer out of him.'

His advice was born of experience, as was shown when he remarked, 'If you three-putt the first green, they'll never remember it. But if you three-putt the eighteenth, they'll never forget it!'

Peter Alliss:

Sam Snead had some delightful little eccentric touches. His trademark was a straw hat with colourful bands; he used to travel with at least half a dozen of them in a long polythene bag. He used to tuck a $100 bill underneath each of the bands. Once, when we were competing in the Canada Cup matches, as they were then called (now the World Cup) in Puerto Rico, he left his beloved hats on the bus. There was panic because Sam knew there was $600 going a-begging. Anyway, they turned up and all was well.

He had another lovely habit of folding a dollar bill up into the smallest square, smaller than I've ever seen. If anyone gave him any service that he quite liked, or he felt obliged to leave a tip, he used to place it in the hand of the waiter or the bell boy, whoever, with the words, 'Here boy, put that in your hollow tooth.' He'd then walk away. The bill was so small it would take some time before it was all smoothed out.

Then of course the recipient saw it wasn't a five or a ten, just a humble one, but it's the thought that counts!

Tony Jacklin:

A Ben Hogan anecdote that often gets told to illustrate his personality is that of Gary Player phoning Hogan to ask him a question of mechanics. I know Gary and I know Gary would have prefaced such a question with a show of respect and homage to Hogan's accomplishments. Gary would have had considerable time to practise how he planned to ask Mr Hogan this question because it took him six hours to get a line through (this was in the 1960s, don't forget). After finally getting through, Gary posed his question. He waited a second.

'What clubs do you play?' Hogan asked Gary sharply, only because he probably already knew the answer, given that Gary by then was one of the world's top half-dozen golfers.

'Dunlop,' replied Gary.

'Right,' Hogan said flatly. 'Why don't you just phone up Mr Dunlop and ask him what you should do.'

Then he hung up!

Robert Sommers:

Watching how female spectators reacted when Arnold Palmer strode past, a member of the gallery at Pittsburgh's Oakmont Country Club during the 1973 US Open turned to a companion and asked, 'Can you imagine being Arnold Palmer . . . and single?'

Barry Johnston:

Greg Norman has long had the nickname of 'The Great White Shark' because of his white-blond hair, his six-foot height and his aggressive style of playing. The Australian won the Open Championship twice, in 1986 and 1993, but he became equally famous for his near-misses and sudden collapses in the other three majors.

As Martin Johnson once put it so memorably, when the pressure is on, 'The Great White Shark has a history of turning into a fish finger!'

Sandy Lyle:

The South African Bobby Locke was Open champion in 1949, 1950, 1952 and 1957 and winner of eighty-one tournaments worldwide, including a remarkable fifteen in the United States.

Whereas Tiger Woods is the epitome of an athlete, even at the peak of his powers Locke, who always looked older than his years, was an incongruous sight with his, let us say, chunky physique, luxuriant moustache, white cap, plus-fours and tie, but could he play golf! After winning his first Open, Locke was invited to take part in a series of challenge matches against Sam Snead in South Africa, where he stunned the American – and all America, for that matter – by winning twelve of their sixteen contests.

Encouraged by that success, Locke travelled to the US the following year and won six of the first nine tournaments he entered, inspiring great resentment among his less-than-welcoming hosts. Locke took his revenge in the quietest way possible when, shortly before returning home to Johannesburg, an interviewer asked him if he had found it difficult to adjust to the US Tour.

'Oh yes,' he replied drily, 'I very nearly lost four of the first five tournaments I played!'

Tom O'Connor:

I have played courses north and south of the border in Ireland. I will always remember one time at Royal Portrush on a day that the heavens forgot. In seven holes we suffered hell, high water, hurricane and rain like bullets on the skin. Soon it was too cold to grip the bag, never mind the clubs, so we decided to creak back to the clubhouse.

As we stood there, wrapping our purple frames around large warming brandies, we watched a video of Seve Ballesteros doing endless tricks with a putter.

I said to my blue-nosed Irish partner, 'Isn't he just wonderful?'

Ken sniffed and said, 'Ah, yes . . . but can he tile a roof?'

Robert Sommers:

After playing in the 1992 Grand Slam of Golf, a competition limited to the winners of the US Open, the British Open, the PGA championship, and the Masters Tournament, Nick Faldo flew to Fort Worth to meet with Ben Hogan.

Like everyone else, Faldo held him in awe. They spent an hour talking. After lunch at Shady Oaks, Faldo asked if he would watch him play some practice shots. Hogan declined. Then Nick asked if Hogan would share a secret with him. Hogan asked, 'What secret?'

'I really want to win the US Open,' Faldo said, 'and I'd like you to tell me the secret to it.'

Hogan said, 'Shoot a lower score than anybody else!'

Barry Johnston:

In January 1994 Jack Nicklaus won the Mercedes Championship in Carlsbad, California, the first official tournament on the Senior PGA Tour, but it was to be his only win of the year. After suffering with his game for several months, the fifty-four-year-old Golden Bear joked, 'People have always said, "Jack, I wish I could play like you." Well, now they can!'

Sandy Lyle:

I uttered one of my classic lines at the 1992 LA Open when a certain sixteen-year-old named Tiger Woods was playing and had just missed the cut. I was in the press tent after finishing my round when one of the journalists asked, 'Sandy, what do you think of Tiger Woods?'

Odd question, I thought, seeing as how we're here at the Riviera Country Club, but all right, I'm always happy to answer.

'Sorry,' I said, 'don't think I've played that course!'

PRO-AM

Sandy Lyle:

Some pros dread the pro-ams, which can make it a very long four or five hours out on the course, but I have always enjoyed the experience and try my best to make sure my partners derive similar enjoyment from our round.

One amateur partner watched me reach a par-four green with a driver and one-iron before casually asking, 'Are you a pro?'

'Yes,' I said. 'As a matter of fact I'm the British Open champion.'

'I thought I recognised the accent!'

Nick Faldo:

America can provide some lighter moments, especially in the pre-tournament pro-am events where anything can, and frequently does, happen. Sometimes you find yourself sharing a round with a low-handicap player who knows his way round a course. More often, however, you are paired with a millionaire businessman who cannot tell his mashie-niblick from his elbow.

On one such afternoon my caddie, Fanny Sunesson, and I stood on the 1st tee beside a young giant of the business world who had the very best clubs, a crocodile skin bag and every gimmick known to the pro shop, including fluorescent coloured golf balls. Orange ball number one was sliced into the trees. That was swiftly followed by a yellow missile, which was hooked into the lake. My companion decided enough was enough and wrote 'no return' on his scorecard. At the second hole it was orange right into trees, yellow left into water – 'no return'.

By the 13th hole he had still not set foot on a green. Belatedly, on the 14th par-three he hit his tee shot a hundred yards or so down the middle – 'Very good,' I said encouragingly – then knocked his approach into a greenside bunker whereupon he picked up his ball and put it in his pocket.

'Aren't you going to play out?' I asked.

'No,' he said. 'Bunker play is not the strong point of my game!'

Peter Dobereiner:

Everybody knows that the greatest glory of the game of golf is a handicapping system that enables the veriest rabbit to play on level terms with Jack Nicklaus. Everybody who has actually put this glory to the test knows it to be a load of cobblers.

However, since there is only one Jack Nicklaus and at a rough count there are some thirty to forty million rabbits, the myth survives and there is never any shortage of romantic fools who believe that their handicap strokes make them the equal of the star tournament players.

Hence the pro-am, a highly refined form of golf torture

whose only merit is that it raises millions and millions of pounds for charity every year.

A non-golfer with a keen grasp of higher mathematics will tell you that the handicap system is foolproof. A 16-handicapper will, by definition, play sixteen strokes more than par and, if he gets his full stroke allowance, as mostly happens in pro-ams, he will have a 72, which is likely to be the score of his pro.

In practice, it does not work like that. What happens is that as soon as the 16-handicapper learns that he has been drawn to play with Sandy Lyle, he breaks into a cold sweat. Strictly speaking, he is clinically mad from now on with a mental derangement known to psychiatrists as Toad of Toad Hall Syndrome. The syndrome includes severe dislocation from reality, fantasies about playing a career best round of 73, less 16, giving a net 57, probably followed by a request from the admiring Lyle to come to the practice ground and pass on a few tips.

The disease now follows a predictable pattern. The victim goes to the pro's shop and splurges on a new colour co-ordinated outfit of shirt, sweater, slacks, glove, cap, pro bag and, the first fatal error, new shoes. The second really disastrous mistake is that he also books up for a lesson. Having guaranteed that he will suffer from blistered heels and that his limited ability will have deteriorated by a minimum of ten strokes a round, he is now ready for the big day.

When they meet on the 1st tee, Lyle could not be more comforting. 'Just play your normal game and don't worry about anything. We'll have a nice, friendly round.' Our poor booby tries to reply but owing to the dryness of his throat his merry quip comes out as a Donald Duck croak. There are, he estimates, some ten thousand spectators gathered around the 1st tee, all of them wearing expressions of mocking amusement.

Something very peculiar is happening to his knees. His name is called and he tees his ball. A sudden spasm afflicts his hands and the ball falls off the tee. Someone in the gallery titters. By the time he straightens up, his hands are trembling uncontrollably, a problem for which there is only one solution. He grasps the driver in a grip so tight that all circulation of blood below the wrist is thwarted. It has to go somewhere and, as he addresses the ball, a red glaze covers his eyes, effectively blinding him.

His rising panic is compounded by the sudden realisation that he has forgotten what he is supposed to do with the golf club. Some vestigial instinct prompts him to raise the driver in the manner of a drunken executioner lifting his sword; in a convulsive spasm he brings it down again. The toe of the driver catches the ball a glancing blow, causing it to shoot off at a right angle and inflict painful shin wounds among the sneering populace.

That tangential cover drive from the 1st tee is a

common opening gambit in pro-ams, but there are several interesting variations: the air shot, the scuttling squirt into the left rough, the swing that passes clean underneath the ball in a flurry of flying turf and tee peg, leaving the ball to drop vertically into the crater. My own speciality used to be the premature evacuation, with the club-head entering the turf eleven inches (my personal best) behind the ball and ploughing onwards with a growing accumulation of grass and dirt pushed by my impromptu bulldozer blade just far enough to topple the ball from its peg.

Anyway, once the pantomime of the opening tee shot is over, things tend to improve and the pro-am amateur should lose no opportunity to pull the integrity ploy. Once you are sure your score cannot contribute to the team's fortunes, call a penalty on yourself, whether or not it is justified, ostentatiously put your ball away and announce: 'I'm afraid you chaps will have to do the business on this hole. Damn ball moved at the address.' You thus create the impression of honest endeavour thwarted by bad luck and, incidentally, contribute to the speed of play.

By such strategy the experienced pro-am hand can contribute not a single point to the team's welfare but win the reputation as a frightfully decent chap, modest and cheerful even though he was dreadfully unlucky with the golf.

Obviously, a pretty useful player, but it was just not his day!

Nick Faldo:

On one occasion I was paired in a pro-am with a little old man in his eighties who hacked his way down the 1st, eventually taking a 10.

'I think this fella needs some help,' I whispered to Fanny Sunesson.

On the 2nd tee, I took him aside and mentioned, as kindly as I could, 'You've got to try and scrape the club away by taking a wider backswing.'

'No, I can't do that. I've just had both hips replaced and I'm still very stiff.'

'Well, try and get your left shoulder under your chin just a little bit.'

'I'm afraid I can't do that either. I've just had a new titanium rotator-cuff put in my shoulder as well.'

'OK, fine, then keep your eyes on the ball as you go through.'

'You're not going to believe this but this morning I picked up my wife's glasses and I'm having trouble focusing on the ball.'

'So, apart from that, everything's all right?'

'Pardon?'

Cue outbreak of hysterics from Ms Sunesson.

Sandy Lyle:

At the Bing Crosby tournament in Pebble Beach one spring, I was fortunate to be paired with the astronaut Alan Shepard. He had smuggled a five-iron and ball aboard Apollo 14 and became the only man since the dawn of time to play golf on the moon, 'hitting it miles and miles and miles . . .'

Alan told me an amusing tale of the night he and fellow astronaut Edgar Mitchell were woken by a strange clanging noise in the lunar module.

'Did you hear that?' Alan whispered.

'Yeah, what do you think it was?' Mitchell replied in a similarly hushed tone.

'I don't know. Neither do I know why we're whispering when the nearest life form – I hope – is a quarter of a million miles away on Earth!'

Ian Wooldridge:

Dateline: Wentworth, 1986
It was like tackling *The Times* crossword in front of Einstein. Or driving James Hunt to the airport. Or writing a letter to Graham Greene.

You know the true giants are invariably tolerant, yet lunch – in this column's case two stiff gins and a bowl of soup – rested in the stomach like suet pudding. One is old enough to recognise the symptoms of a bad attack of nerves.

At 2.42 p.m. precisely the starter at Wentworth's Burma Road calls this column's name with all the enthusiasm of an auctioneer selling off a job lot of back copies of *Farmers' Weekly*. One steps forward, waxen-smiled, armed with a four-iron.

As anyone who knows anything about golf will tell you, a four-iron is probably the most stupid club a man can carry on to what the critics have called the most intimidating 1st tee in Britain. Even if stupendously struck, it will hardly get you into competitive play on this switchback par-four.

Why, then, take a four-iron? Because it is the only club with which your correspondent, an occasional golfer, can make contact with the ball on a reasonably regular basis.

Shrewd thinking, though I say it myself. The usual purple mists cloud the brain at the top of the backswing but somehow the ball flies 170 yards straight as an arrow into a fearful lie in some transverse rough.

Like every amateur who has ever played in a pro-am we thank Our Maker for sparing us an air swing.

Proceeding down the fairway, an arm falls lightly round my shoulder.

'Why you hit four-iron?' he say.

'Because,' I say, lapsing into the pidgin-speech we British use instead of foreign languages, 'I no good with any other club.'

'Rubbish,' says Severiano Ballesteros, the best golfer in the world. 'You just stand up there and hit the ball with any bloody club you please. We all friends here, unnerstand?'

This you are not going to believe. Our foursome, also involving Dennis Hart, a Scottish travel agent, and Ian Chubb, a Bell's Whisky man, all got down in five at the first hole. So did Seve, who may well deliberately have punched his second shot left of the green to make the rest of us feel better.

At the short 5th, we halve another in par. 'Estupendo,' he cry. We are feeling better now.

The knees have stopped quivering and mists are clearing. This was Seve's being-nice day to the public.

Ballesteros flew in to Wentworth by helicopter. Since he's staying in a not-distant hotel for this weekend's European event at Sunningdale, he could, possibly more swiftly and certainly at one-tenth of the price, have come by car.

But it was a day for style, not economy. When the rotor blades stopped he stepped out to devote an entire day to publicising the La Manga Club, a sports resort in South East Spain, to which he is attached as travelling professional. It involves playing golf with the likes of me.

He chats amiably along the fairway. 'No,' he says, 'I no learn a single word of English until I seventeen. Then I began to travel and picked up a few words.' He now speaks English engagingly. 'No problem' is his favourite phrase.

'No problem,' he laughs as you hook another tee shot into foliage. 'Funny game is golf. It's the only sport which the professionals practise all the time and the amateurs never practise at all. Do you practise?'

'Never,' I admit.

'Yes, I can see that,' he says. 'Me, I am like a pianist. When I am not playing in tournaments I still practise six, seven hours every day. It is the only way I know to stay where I am.'

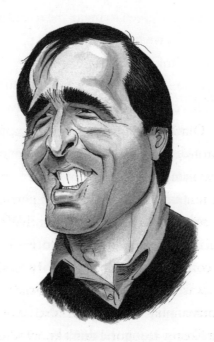

The great man demonstrated the controlled draw and slice, issued a few tips, signed autographs and dispensed bonhomie all day, earning in the process slightly more than Max Faulkner won in prize money during his entire career!

ST ANDREWS

Barry Johnston:

José Maria Olazábal may appear relaxed playing in front of a large gallery at a golf tournament but when it comes to making a speech, it is a different matter. At the Association of Golf Writers' annual dinner in St Andrews in 2000, Olazábal explained the reason for his nerves. 'The faraway bull in the field looks very small. But when it comes close you think, "My God!"'

When he was presented with an award at the PGA European Tour annual dinner, Olazábal apologised, 'This speech is a bit like my tee shot. I don't know where it's going!'

Barry Johnston:

Even though it was his first visit to St Andrews, Tony Lema quickly mastered the intricacies of the Old Course, and the former US Marine was the unexpected winner of the 1964 Open Championship. The runner-up was Jack Nicklaus, who had been hindered by the extremely windy conditions on the first day. Despite posting two final rounds of 66 and 68, Nicklaus succeeded only in reducing Lema's winning margin to five shots.

Back in the R&A clubhouse a journalist said to Nicklaus, 'I see, Jack, you've discovered the secret of the Old Course.'

'Yeah,' replied Nicklaus laconically. 'Fewer putts!'

Peter Dobereiner:

Once upon a time the championship committee of the Royal and Ancient Golf Club of St Andrews was made up of trusting men who took the world at face value. No trace of cynicism tainted their natures. In their own circle if a chap said he was eight-handicap, a chap did not have to ask the chap to produce a handicap certificate because a chap's word was a sacred bond. Dammit, if a chap couldn't trust a chap then what would the world be coming to, eh?

Thus it came about that when an entry was received for the 1965 Open Championship from Walter Danecki of Milwaukee, his name went straight into the draw for qualifying rounds. After all, the chap described himself as a professional golfer on the entry form, plain as day.

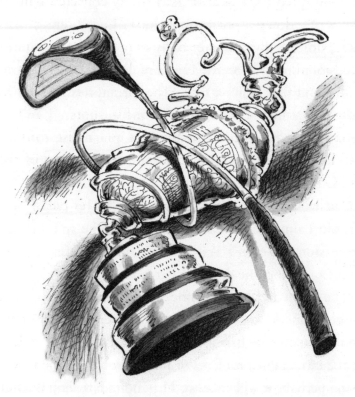

Danecki's appearance at Hillside caused no comment. He looked as much like a golfer as anyone else, a strapping six-footer of some forty-three summers. However, as soon as he swung a club it became obvious that Walter had not devoted too many of those summers to perfecting the arts of the royal and ancient game. He breezed around Hillside in a cool 108, a score that aroused the curiosity of the ever-alert golfing press.

Danecki explained that in fact he was a mail sorter

'but I wanted the crock of gold so my conscience made me write down "professional"'. His golf credentials were, admittedly, meagre, consisting of seven years of occasional rounds over his local municipal course at one dollar and fifty cents a time. The formalities for joining the PGA were too complicated and protracted and so he hit upon this idea of the British Open to cut through the red tape. He reasoned, 'What I will do is win one of the big ones and then they will have to let me in.' He added that he was self-taught, thought he could beat Arnold Palmer, and that he adhered to the spirit of the Professional Golfer's Association rules insofar as, not being a member, he did not charge for lessons.

The Royal and Ancient officials pondered the subject of Walter Danecki and came up with the statesmanlike solution that successive British governments had applied to most of the intractable problems of international affairs: ignore it and perhaps it will go away. They nominated a substitute to take Danecki's place in the second round, confident that he would lose no time in returning to Milwaukee.

Alas for their optimism, Danecki reported to the tee for his second round, eager to repair the damage of that opening 108. He said, 'I don't like to quit. I like golf. That's what I came here to do.' He started, 7, 7, 8, and then, as the Americans say, the wheels came off and he scored 113, giving him a total that failed to qualify for the Open Championship by 75 strokes.

There is not, you might think, much that a golfer can say of a positive, heartening nature after such a performance. Walter was up to the challenge of the moment. He said: 'I want to say that your small ball is right for this sort of course. If I had been playing our bigger ball, I would have been all over the place.'

All in all, he conceded, he was slightly discouraged by the events of these two days because, after all, he had been after the money!

Barry Johnston:

The Australian golfer Peter Thomson won five Open titles between 1954 and 1965, including three in consecutive years. He went on to enjoy a successful career on the Senior PGA Tour and has designed many golf courses in Australia.

Thomson's second Open win was on the Old Course at St Andrews and, talking about the event many years later, he said, 'The Road Hole, the seventeenth, is the most famous and infamous hole. As a planner and builder of golf holes worldwide, I have no hesitation in allowing that if one built such a hole today, you would be sued for incompetence!'

Barry Johnston:

The American professional Boo Weekley is the first to admit that the history of the game is not exactly his strong point, even though he was a hero of the winning United States team in the 2008 Ryder Cup. When Weekley visited Scotland in 2007 to play in his first Open Championship at Carnoustie, he was asked if he was going to visit the home of golf at St Andrews.

The American looked puzzled. He proclaimed, 'I didn't know it was the home of golf. I thought the home of golf was where I was from!'

Barry Johnston:

In 1954, when the Canadian team turned up to play at St Andrews in a Commonwealth golf tournament, one of their members was wearing a plaid lumberjack shirt. He attracted the attention of the veteran golf writer Bernard Darwin, who was less than impressed.

Darwin, a former captain of the Royal and Ancient, asked drily, 'Are those your old school colours or your own unfortunate choice?'

Sandy Lyle:

One of my favourite stories, which underlines the importance of paying the caddie a decent tip, tells of an incident at the end of a round at St Andrews when the golfer gave his caddie three pennies. The caddie laid them in his palm, saying to the player, 'Sir, are ye

aware I can tell yer fortune from these three coins?'
The caddie went on to volunteer that the first one told
him, 'Yer no' a Scotsman,' to which the golfer nodded
assent. 'An' the second that yer no' married,' continued the caddie, to which the golfer nodded as well,
asking about the third.

'Weel, the third wan tells me that your father wisnae
married either!'

Frank Keating:

On 13 July 1970 the popular American Doug Sanders,
a colourful chap in both dress and spirit who called his
autobiography *Come Swing With Me*, had a last-hole putt
to win the Open – and on the High Altar of St Andrews
of all places. This day he was dressed all in purple, both
trews and pullover. He needed a par-four up the 18th and
the jug was his, and he'd done everything right because
here he was with a cinch of a putt for his four. He settled
his expensive black alligator-shoes alongside the ball and
bent over his putter. He was ready for immortality.

Of a sudden, he seemed to notice something – was it an
imaginary wormcast, one blade of razor-shaved grass the
roller had missed, one infinitesimal grain of sand? Without
changing the position of his feet, he bent to brush it away
with no more than a momentary flick of his right hand.
With the soles of his shoes still rooted to the exact same

position, he now resettled over the ball – and as he did so, the BBC TV's doyen commentator Henry Longhurst gave a gasp and a murmured 'Oh, no' – and those in the know in the multi-million audience watching live around the world realised what Henry meant. He meant that Sanders had not reset his stance. He should have stood up, walked away, relaxed again, and then resettled.

Instead, he pulled back his putter and – gently gently now – he jabbed at it. Oh, no . . . In the same twitch, Sanders on reflex tried to reach out with his club towards the ball to rake it back and have another go. There was no second go. The little dimpled onion, taunting him, rolled slowly four inches to the right-hand side of the hole and past it . . . 'Oh, there but for the grace of God . . .' murmured the croaky Longhurst to the world.

A bogey five meant a play-off with Jack Nicklaus next day, which Sanders lost by a stroke, 73–72. But the one shot that lost it had been the day before. Sanders tied for second in four majors. He never did win one.

'No, sir,' he told me exactly twenty years later to the week, 'I don't think about St Andrews very much at all – only about every three minutes every day of my life!'

Barry Johnston:

The Canadian golfer Richard Zokol fell victim to the notorious Road Hole at St Andrews during the

1986 Alfred Dunhill Cup. After Zokol had tried and failed several times to escape from the fearsome Road bunker, Peter Alliss cast an amused eye over the scene of destruction.

'My, my,' he told his television audience, 'it looks like a couple of Shetland ponies have been mating in there!'

John Daly:

The happiest four days of my life in golf were the four days of the 1995 British Open at St Andrews. I won the tournament after beating Costantino Rocca in a four-hole playoff, and when me and my posse were done hugging and kissing and jumping around like idiots, my agent, Bud Martin, got a call from Wilson and Reebok, my two biggest sponsors at the time. They wanted me to get back down to Swilcan Bridge as soon as I could. They had photographers all lined up and ready to go, and they wanted pictures of me on the bridge with the Royal and Ancient clubhouse in the background. But they wanted me, like, *right now*, because the light was only going to be good for a little while longer.

Swilcan Bridge is the bridge that crosses the creek – sorry, Swilcan Burn – that runs across the 1st and 18th fairways. It's like 500 years old or something, and is one of the most famous spots in golf. On Friday, Arnold Palmer, who was making his last appearance in a British Open, stopped on that bridge to wave one last goodbye.

But before I could go down for the photo shoot, me and Costantino had to submit our scorecards, and then there was the presentation of the claret jug on the 18th green, and I had to say something without bawling like a baby. So by the time we finished everything, the sun was dropping, and the Wilson and Reebok people were going nuts.

So Bud and I hustled over to a golf cart and started out for Swilcan Bridge, when all of a sudden somebody came running out of the media room yelling, 'Stop! You got to come back! You got to come back! The President's on the phone! He wants to talk to you!'

My first thought is, holy shit, the President of the United States wants to talk to me. But then Bud pointed out that Wilson and Reebok were putting about $4 million a year in my pocket, and all Clinton was doing was taking 40 per cent of that away, and that the sun was just about to sink behind the Old Course Hotel. It was now or never for the commemorative photo. So, talk to Clinton or pose for the photo? It didn't take me long to figure out what to do: 'Hit it, Bud.'

We get the photo shoot done with about a minute to spare.

Later that night, when we got back to our rooms in the Old Course Hotel, there were a bunch of new messages, including one that said: 'Please call the President of the United States.'

Fine, I said. I get the picture, and I will. But I still haven't had dinner yet, and I'm starving. Besides, I didn't even vote for the guy. But now Bud's going the other way: 'He's the president, John. You've got to talk to him. Please! Do it now.'

So I'm like, okay, okay, get him on the horn, only that turned out to take a lot of back-and-forth, one guy talking to another guy who told me to hold on, all this even though he'd been the one to call me in the first place. But finally a guy came on and said, 'John, this is President Clinton.'

Sure it was – I recognised the voice right off. You can take the boy out of Arkansas, but you can't take Arkansas out of the boy. And so I said, 'Thanks for calling. Sorry it took me a while to get back to you.' And then we went back and forth a little: how do you feel, were you blown away when Rocca made that putt, you made us all proud, blah-blah-blah. And about then I recalled something: 'Say, do you remember that time we played golf after I won the PGA and you were still governor? Well, you told me you'd look into a speeding ticket I got that time outside of Fort Smith the month before, only you didn't, and it's costing me two grand a year on my insurance!'

So he laughed this big laugh, and said he's sorry, but he can't do anything about it now because he's not governor

86

anymore. And then he congratulated me again, and we shot the shit some more, and I thanked him, and we said goodbye.

It was pretty nice, if you think about it. After all, here's the President of the United States, a fellow Arkansas boy, calling to say he's proud of me for winning a damned golf tournament.

Pretty nice, but I didn't vote for him the second time around either!

AMERICAN TALES

Nick Faldo:

While I was in the USA in 1991 I was invited to a White House reception hosted by President George Bush in honour of Margaret Thatcher, who was due to receive the Medal of Freedom. President Bush was the latest in a long line of White House residents who were also passionate golfers, and possessed a vast repertoire of yarns involving his predecessors.

Did you know, for instance, that when asked why he had given up golf for oil painting, Dwight D. Eisenhower replied, 'Because I take less strokes with a brush!'

Barry Johnston:

Bing Crosby and Bob Hope co-starred in seven classic comedy films, from *Road to Singapore* in 1940 to *The Road to Hong Kong* in 1962. The films were notable for the pair's quickfire humour and their playful competitiveness, which extended to their love of golf.

Hope was an avid golfer and the comedian was quoted as saying, 'Golf is my profession. I tell jokes to pay my green fees!'

Bing Crosby and Bob Hope each founded their own golf tournaments in the United States, raising millions of dollars for charity, but could never resist taking a swipe at the other's golfing prowess. Crosby was once asked what he thought of his friend's swing.

He laughed. 'Bob Hope's swing? I've seen better swings on a condemned playground!'

Bruce Forsyth:

I must own up to some odd encounters and embarrassing moments on the course. Perhaps the oddest was when I was playing the water hole in Palm Springs. This is a short hole, over the water and you have about a 140-yard carry before you get to the green. It's quite a tricky hole. All my three partners had played, so I got set up, addressed the ball, took the club back.

I was at the top of my swing when . . . a frogman came out of the water! I mean he shot out of the water like a killer whale. My club went flying and my three friends were in hysterics.

I nearly had a heart attack!

Barry Johnston:

During the second round of the 1975 Western Open at the Butler National Golf Club in Oak Brook, Illinois, a sudden thunderstorm forced play to be suspended. Lee Trevino and his playing partner, a promising young professional called Jerry Heard, took shelter under an umbrella on the edge of the 13th green, alongside Teal Lake, while they waited for the shower to pass.

Suddenly, a lightning bolt flashed across the water, surged through Trevino's bag, up his arm and out of his back. Both golfers were thrown into the air. Trevino joked later, 'When God wants to play through, you'd better step aside!' He required two spinal operations, but recovered. Nine of his career total of twenty-seven victories on the PGA Tour came after the event.

This was the second time Trevino had been struck by lightning while playing golf. The odds against that happening are meant to be nine million to one, so 'Super Mex' knows what he is talking about when he advises, 'If you are caught on a golf course during a storm and are afraid of lightning, hold up a one-iron. Not even God can hit a one-iron!'

Robert Sommers:

Jim Thorpe was about to win the 1985 Greater Milwaukee Open, his first victory as a professional. He was paired with Jack Nicklaus in the last round and led Jack by three strokes as they walked down the 18th fairway.

Realising that anything could happen, Jack tried to shake Thorpe's confidence and upset his composure. 'How does it feel to be walking down the last fairway with a three-shot lead over the greatest player the game has ever known?' he needled.

Without missing a step, Thorpe smirked, 'It feels like you can't win!'

Barry Johnston:

South African Simon Hobday spent most of his professional career on the Southern African Tour, although he also won the 1976 German Open and the 1979 Madrid Open. As a senior he played on the Champions Tour in the United States, where he was the surprise winner of the 1994 US Senior Open at the Pinehurst Country Club, in North Carolina.

As he walked up the 18th fairway at Pinehurst, Hobday was so nervous that he put his hands around his throat to demonstrate that he was choking. Afterwards he admitted, 'I'm a renowned choker from way back. I choked all the way through to the last putt!'

Hobday, known as 'Scruffy' because of his unkempt appearance, once sent two balls into the water and announced, 'By God, I've got a good mind to jump in and make it four!'

Michael Green: The Art of Coarse Golf

I am indebted to an old friend, Mr Richard Field, of Northampton, for a description of the most unusual hazard I have ever heard of.

While playing at a course in Arizona, he noticed that players who hit balls into a shallow water hazard never bothered to collect them.

Being a hard-up Englishman he therefore paddled in and began to fill his bag when he was arrested by an armed sheriff patrolling the course with two six-guns and a ten-gallon hat.

Perhaps the fact that Richard greeted him by saying, 'Where did you come from? A cornflake packet?' may have had something to do with it.

The sheriff could not believe that anyone would want to waste time salvaging a lost ball and decided that the English Coarse Golfers must have been connected with Communism.

Richard explained that Englishmen always salvage any balls they can, as so many are lost due to the fog, which permanently envelops the country, and he was released with a warning.

Barry Johnston:

The cowboy and humorist Will Rogers was the most popular American radio personality of the early 1930s. He never understood the appeal of golf. He said, 'I have never been depressed enough to take up the game but they say you get so sore at yourself you forget to hate your enemies!'

He once joked, 'Seeing a man walking around a golf course hitting a ball is like somebody handling a ukelele. You can't tell whether they are playing it or just monkeying around!'

When he was asked his opinion of golf, Rogers said, 'I am not going to make the mistake of the usual fool (just because I don't play the game) and tell you there is nothing to it. There is skill in anything, if you practise it long enough. Spitting at a crack don't get much recognition among the Arts, but you just try to hit one some time and you will never laugh at another spitter.'

He quipped, 'The main thing that struck me about the game was the amount of skill they had developed in getting near the hole and how little they displayed in getting into it!'

Rogers was baffled by the rules of golf. He said, 'It's the only game outside of solitaire where you play alone. What you do with your ball hasn't got anything to do with what the other fellow does with his. I can play in the morning and you [can play] a month from now. There is a pardner, or accomplice, who plays along with you. You are not sent out for company but to annoy each other. Then when you get through the game the strain is not over. You have to wait till the last guy comes in at sundown to find out what happened to you!'

Sandy Lyle:

Former US President Gerald Ford was a serious public nuisance in any pro-celebrity event. Bob Hope would weave an entire stand-up routine around poor Gerry's reputation as the least expert golfer in the world:

- He'd give up golf if he didn't have so many nice sweaters.
- The last time I played a round with Gerald Ford he hit one birdie, an eagle, a jack-rabbit, an elk and three pensioners.

- There are forty-two golf courses in Palm Springs and President Ford waits until he hits his first drive before announcing which one he's playing that day.
- When Russian premier Andrei Gromyko gets down to disarmament talks, the first item on his agenda will be taking away Mr Ford's clubs.
- He's the most dangerous driver since Ben Hur.
- It's not hard to find the President on the course – you just follow the walking wounded.
- And on the 1st tee, Gerry Ford, the man who has made golf a contact sport and with whom the word 'Fore!' is synonymous!

Barry Johnston:

Bob Shearer won twenty tournaments on the PGA Tour of Australia between 1974 and 1986, topping the Order of Merit four times, but he was unable to repeat his success abroad. Although Shearer moved his family from Melbourne to live in the United States, he achieved only one victory in the nine years he spent on the US PGA Tour.

In 1980 the Australian was taking part in the Atlanta Classic at Marietta, Georgia, when his loyal wife, Kathy, rang the Atlanta Country Club to see how he was getting on. She enquired how many Bob Shearer had shot and was told, 'Sixty-three, Ma'am.'

There was a short pause, before Kathy repeated, 'No, Shearer. That's S - H - E - A - R - E - R!'

John Daly:

Every year, usually the Monday and Tuesday after the International in Castle Pines, Colorado, Peter Jacobsen used to host this great charity event in Portland called the Fred Meyer Challenge. It always attracted a great field because Peter's such a great host. He threw this great party every year where he and his band, Jake Trout and the Flounders, would entertain about a thousand people in this humongous tent with some good old rock-and-roll.

But even more fun was the 'golf clinic' Peter put on for the fans before the tournament. People jammed temporary grandstands behind the 1st tee, and Peter stood on the tee box and did this funny-ass routine where he mimicked the swings of a lot of the guys. Then, with everybody in a good mood, he'd bring out a few pros to demonstrate different kinds of shots – you know, a cut, a draw, a banana slice, a straight-up L-wedge, that sort of thing. It gave the crowd a good demonstration, and it gave us a chance to show off.

As you'd figure, Peter asked me to come out and demonstrate hitting a driver. He set me up real good, cracking jokes about this and that, and I played along because I wanted to put on a good show for the fans. Only when I went to hit my drive, I turned around and set up facing the fans in the stands. I made a big production of it, taking my time, loosening up my shoulders, and waggling my Killer Whale (the Wilson driver I used at the time). The fans were cheering and whooping and eating it up. Kill it, Big John! Grip it and rip it! One guy in the back row, he stood up and held his arms up like he was a goalpost. And so I stood up to the ball and let 'er rip.

I think everybody thought it was going to be one of those fake exploding balls. It wasn't. It was one of my John Daly Wilson Staff signature babies, and I caught it good. It cleared the stands by a good fifty feet – splitting the uprights – and ended up in the parking lot about 300 yards away.

People went nuts. They loved it.

Deane Beman, the commissioner of the PGA Tour, went nuts too. Only he hated it.

'John, that'll cost you $30,000.'

P.S. The next year, we did use one of those fake exploding golf balls. People didn't like it half as much!

Barry Johnston:

Steve Melnyk, from Brunswick, Georgia, won both the 1969 US Amateur Championship and the 1971 British Amateur Championship and played twice on the American team in the Walker Cup.

Unfortunately, Melnyk was less successful as a professional and he never won a tournament on the US PGA Tour. On one occasion he flew four thousand miles to play in the Hawaiian Open. When he landed in Hawaii, he discovered he had forgotten to enter for the tournament!

Sandy Lyle:

Chi Chi Rodriguez is a one-off and no mistake. A child at heart, he says his proudest achievement is not the £7 million plus he has earned through golf but the Chi Chi Rodriguez Youth Foundation in Clearwater, Florida, a refuge for abused and troubled kiddies.

Born in Rio Piedras, Puerto Rico, Chi Chi began caddying as a six-year-old and taught himself to play using 'clubs' fashioned from guava tree branches and 'balls' made out of tin cans, which he would hammer into as round a shape as possible. 'I could hit that thing a hundred yards but it never was much good for putting. That's OK. I never liked putting anyway. Putting isn't golf. It should be treated the same as a water hazard . . . hit it on and add two strokes.'

Despite his slender physique and lack of height – 'When I first came on the Tour, my playing partners would use me as a ball marker' – Chi Chi could smash the ball a country mile and more, a talent for which he had another ready-made quip. 'I once hit a drive five hundred yards – on a par-three. I had a three-wood coming back!' Boy, was he straight off the tee. 'The last time I left the fairway was to answer the telephone, and it was a wrong number!'

Chi Chi's bag came equipped with all manner of stage-props for his one-man show. One of his favourite routines on the 1st tee, which I have witnessed, much to my amusement, involved asking the gallery if they had seen the newest Puerto Rican credit card. Whereupon he would delve into his clubs and produce a flick-knife.

Chi Chi was proud of his heritage but never passed up an opportunity to make fun of his nationality. Partnered by Homero Blancas, another Latino, and Rod Curl, who is a Native American, at one tournament, he offered the immortal observation, 'It looked like a Civil Rights march out there. People thought we were going to steal their hubcaps. After all these years it's still embarrassing for me to play in America. Like the time I asked my caddie for a sand-wedge and he came back with a ham on rye!'

Barry Johnston:

There must be something about golf and American politicians, especially members of the Republican Party.

After Spiro T. Agnew, then vice president to Richard Nixon, had finished his round in the 1972 Bob Hope Desert Classic, he was complimented by journalists on his improved game.

Agnew told them proudly, 'I don't think I played better. I just missed more people!'

Sam Torrance:

Fellow pro Simon Hobday tells a story about when he was travelling late to an event in the States and was stopped on the freeway going at 110mph. Simon pulled over and saw a huge macho American cop strolling towards his car.

The cop bent down towards Simon and drawled, 'Goddam my boy – I have been waiting all day for someone like you,' to which Simon replied, 'Well, I got here as quick as I could!'

Tom O'Connor:

When John Jacobs went to America for the first time to do golf commentaries, he did not appreciate that Americans have different terminologies from ours. This guy had hit his ball out of the bunker and taken no sand, just flicked it off the top. Over here we would call that a 'pecker' (like a chicken pecking corn), which of course has a totally different connotation in the States. So when John said, 'This man looks like a pecker,' they gave him some very odd looks. It all went very quiet in the box.

Then John turned to his companion in the commentary box and confided, 'Can't wait for the commercial break. I'm dying for a fag.'

That was his reputation gone up in smoke!

Barry Johnston:

After he won the 1993 PGA Grand Slam at La Quinta, California, with a 1-over-par, Greg Norman picked up a winner's cheque of $400,000, the biggest cheque in his seventeen-year career. But the Great White Shark was not entirely happy with his performance.

Describing his play afterwards, Norman said, 'It was like a mackerel in the moonlight – shiny one minute and smelly the next!'

Ian Woosnam:

By 1987, the significance of my Welshness seemed somehow index-linked to my success in the game. The more I won, the more people seemed to know where I came from and, consequently, the more proud I felt to call myself a Welshman.

'So, Woosie, you're from Wales?' an American journalist asked me during a press conference that year.

'That's right,' I replied.

'So what part of Scotland is that?'

OPEN CHAMPIONSHIP

Tony Jacklin:

Royal Lytham has a fantastic history I'm proud to be part of. It hosted its first Open in 1926, and this was the Open in which the great Bobby Jones, in the course of winning, retired to his hotel for lunch between the third and fourth rounds (both being played on the Saturday at the time). He went back to the course after lunch to play the final round. An entrance man stopped him at the gate and said he'd have to pay a fee to get back in.

'But I'm leading the tournament!' said Jones.

The entrance man was unmoved and Jones had to come up with his two shillings and sixpence (12 ½ p) just for the privilege of going back in to win the tournament!

Barry Johnston:

Mark Calcavecchia won his only major at the 1989 Open Championship at Royal Troon after a four-hole playoff with Wayne Grady and Greg Norman. When he was awarded the claret jug, Calcavecchia – whose lengthy Italian surname means 'old crowd' – enquired of an official, 'How's my name going to fit on that thing!'

Two years later, after shooting a 79 in the second round of the 1991 Open at Royal Birkdale, Calcavecchia was leaving the course when he suddenly handed his clubs to a golf course attendant. 'Take 'em,' he said.

The surprised attendant asked what he was going to use the next day.

Calcavecchia replied, 'The airplane. I've missed the cut!'

Robert Sommers:

Not exempt in 1992, Ben Crenshaw had to qualify for the Open, but he shot 79 in the first round and lost his chance of winning a place in the field.

Later that afternoon he slunk onto a stool in the small bar at Greywalls, the hotel alongside Muirfield. The bartender approached and asked, 'What can I bring you, sir?'

Glancing up, the sad looking Crenshaw muttered, 'Arsenic!'

Barry Johnston:

Thomas Brent 'Boo' Weekley has become one of the most popular players on the US PGA Tour, where golf fans have warmed to his homespun Southern personality and his country charm. Born in Milton, on the Florida panhandle, the outdoorsman and hunter acquired his nickname from the cartoon hero Yogi Bear's sidekick, Boo Boo Bear. Although he is considered to be one of the purest strikers of the ball in the game, Weekley openly admits that he would often rather be out on his bass boat in Florida than playing golf. He says, 'I love to play the game, but my heart is really with huntin' and fishin'.' He is even sponsored by an outdoor clothing company that specialises in camouflage hunting gear.

When Weekley played in the 2007 Open Championship at Carnoustie, it was not only his first Open but his first trip overseas. He was especially nervous about flying over the Atlantic. He declared, 'All I know is when I get on that airplane, I want a raft under me so if it does decide to go in some water I want to be able to have a fighting chance to get home!'

After arriving in Scotland, Weekley was confused by the unfamiliar food. He said, 'It's rough. It's different eating here than it is at the house. Ain't got no sweet tea and ain't got no fried chicken.' One of his biggest challenges was understanding the menu in his hotel. He revealed, 'I only stick to things I can spell.'

When the golfer was asked if he knew what a haggis was, he answered, 'I ain't got a clue, but I tried it.'

He added grimly, 'I didn't like it, neither!'

Sandy Lyle:

If Tom Weiskopf had realised what a truly great player he was, he would have won far more majors than the 1973 Troon Open, but he appeared to regard himself as being forever in the shadow of Jack Nicklaus, a fellow graduate of Ohio State University. Runner-up four times in the Masters and second again in the 1976 US Open, it was cruelly said of Weiskopf that he knew more ways to choke than Dracula. I always thought that Dracula bit his victims rather than throttled them but there you go . . . Tom never took himself or the game too seriously. In fact, when he became a course designer at the end of his playing days, his wife, Jeanne, commented, 'It's the first job he's had since we were married.'

Talking to J.C. Snead one time, Weiskopf mused, 'Wouldn't it be great if you could come out here and just pick the tournaments you like to play, never practise, hang out in the bars and have a couple of drinks and simply have fun,' to which came the response, 'Tom, that's what you've done your whole life!'

At the 1979 Open at Royal Lytham, Weiskopf was enduring a miserable round when, on a whim, he decided to hit his 80-yard approach to the 16th with his putter before repairing to the bar of the Clifton Hotel. Tom was enjoying a beer when Nicklaus walked up to ask if what he had heard was true.

'Well, Jack,' replied Tom, trying and failing to keep a straight face, 'I wanted to keep the ball under the wind.'

Nicklaus turned those famous ice-blue eyes on his friend, shook his head resignedly, and departed!

Barry Johnston:

Ernie Els made his Open Championship debut at Royal Troon in 1989. The tall South African with the apparently effortless swing was only nineteen and his elder brother, Dirk, was acting as his caddie. At one hole, Dirk suggested a four-iron. The ball soared high over the green and Ernie, known as 'The Big Easy', did his best to remain calm.

'What was that?' he enquired casually of his brother.

Dirk flipped desperately through his yardage book, before exclaiming, 'Oh, jeez, Ernie, I'm on the wrong hole!'

Peter Dobereiner:

After the American mail sorter Walter Danecki hood-winked the championship committee of the R&A and played in a qualifying round of the 1965 Open Championship, steps were taken to ensure that such an embarrassing fiasco could never happen again. Really? Eleven years later another entry from a professional escaped the scrutiny of the committee.

Maurice Flitcroft, a forty-six-year-old crane driver from Barrow-in-Furness, had set his heart on winning the old claret jug and the fortune and glory that went with it. His apprenticeship for the qualifying ordeal was even sketchier than Danecki's, for his association with the game was both brief and nominal. He had taken up golf eighteen months previously and his experience was limited to hitting shots on the beach. When he was called to the tee at Formby for the first qualifying round he was embarking on the first 18 holes of his life.

On the first two holes his marker lost count of Maurice's earnest endeavours and gave him the benefit of the doubt, marking him for an 11 and a 12. The total came to 121 and Maurice put his finger squarely on the problem. He said: 'At the start I was trying too hard. By the end of the round I felt that I was beginning to put it all together.' The evidence supported his diagnosis since his halves read 61, 60. This time the R&A was spared further embarrassment. Flitcroft withdrew from the competition with dignity, saying: 'I have no chance of qualifying.'

A reporter who went to the Flitcroft home that evening said to his mother: 'I have called about Maurice and the Open Championship.'

'Oh yes,' she replied with excitement. 'Has he won?'

Barry Johnston:

When sixty-five-year-old Gary Player walked onto the last green at Royal Lytham during the 2001 Open, the South African veteran was greeted with sustained applause by the spectators in the grandstands. Describing Player's majestic procession past his cheering fans, Peter Alliss told television viewers, 'Here he comes . . . the Queen Mother of golf. All he needs is a couple of corgis!'

Robert Sommers:

Four strokes behind Sandy Lyle after 71 holes of the 1985 Open, Peter Jacobsen had missed the final green at Royal St George's. He had no chance to win, but he would finish as well as he could.

Just as he was about to play a little chip, he spotted a male streaker breaking out of the crowd and running across the green in front of the thousands of spectators crowding the tall bleachers. Calling on his American football background, Jacobsen reacted quickly and levelled the streaker with a first-class tackle.

Denying any sense of outrage, Jacobsen explained he had only one reason for bringing the streaker down. 'He was about to run across the line of my shot.'

He also said, 'I put my shoulder in where it hurt the most!'

Barry Johnston:

During the 2001 Open Championship at Royal Lytham and St Annes the British amateur champion, Michael Hoey, was caddied by his elder brother, Edward. Hoey, from Ballymoney in Northern Ireland, was leaving nothing to chance.

As he negotiated his way round Lytham's narrow fairways he told his brother, 'Punch me if I go for the driver!'

Nick Faldo:

Since time immemorial, caddies have been a breed apart, a law unto themselves. One of Jack Nicklaus's favourite yarns concerns a practice round at Troon in the company of Tom Weiskopf before the 1973 Open. On one of the par-threes, Weiskopf hit a soaring tee shot that bounced once and dropped into the cup for a hole-in-one. Arriving on the green, Nicklaus looked over at a laconic twosome, idly sitting on a wall, cloth caps pulled down over their eyes, and enveloped in a private cloud of roll-up cigarette smoke.

'Did you see Mr Weiskopf's shot?' enquired Jack.

'Aye, that we did, son,' came the reply.

'Well, don't you think it was worth a round of applause?'

'Why? He was only practising, wasn't he?'

Barry Johnston:

Simon Hobday used to believe that God was deliberately picking on him on the golf course. After missing some critical putts during the 1983 Open at Royal Birkdale, he surprised members in the crowded clubhouse when he looked up and cried, 'Why don't You come down and fight like a man?'

At another tournament he wore a Mexican sombrero so that the Heavenly Father could not see him.

Unfortunately, his brilliant strategy did not work. After taking three putts at the 7th, he exclaimed, 'It took seven holes, but You still recognised me!'

Sandy Lyle:

Although never considered one of the game's greats, Craig Stadler was a vastly underrated golfer who won the Masters in 1982, when he also topped the US money-winners' list. That gives some idea of his credentials.

He might also have won the Open on two occasions. He walked up the 72nd fairway in the final pairing, both times ending in disappointment. 'The Walrus' invariably had a smile on his face, though, even at the Sandwich Open of 1985 when he and Jack Nicklaus both shot 83 in the first round. The Golden Bear then went round in 66 against Stadler's 67 to make the cut by one shot. As Stadler tells it, he returned to his hotel after the first round to find his wife, Sue, shaking her head.

'Hey, the great Jack Nicklaus shot eighty-three as well, don't forget,' he was moved to protest. Sue was less than impressed that her hubby was trailing in about 150th place. 'You beat two people!'

Stadler gained a reputation for being a firebrand on the course – asked why he was playing with a new putter on one occasion, he replied, 'Because the old one didn't float!'

Barry Johnston:

Halfway through his round during the 1994 Open at Turnberry, David Feherty needed to relieve himself and he disappeared behind some rocks below the 9th tee. As he was returning, he met the journalist Martin Johnson and warned him, 'Be careful down there. It's playing against the wind!'

P.G. Wodehouse: The Salvation of George Mackintosh

The finest golfers are always the least loquacious. It is related of the illustrious Sandy McHoots that when, on the occasion of his winning the British Open Championship, he was interviewed by reporters from the leading daily papers as to his views on Tariff Reform, Bimetallism, the Trial by Jury System, and the Modern Craze for Dancing, all they could extract from him was the single word, 'Mphm!' Having uttered which, he shouldered his bag and went home to tea.

A great man. I wish there were more like him!

Barry Johnston:

Ian Poulter has sometimes made more of an impact with his flamboyant clothes on the golf course than with his game. He says, 'The reason I dress the way I do is because I like clothing. I looked down the range this morning and all I saw was black, khaki and navy trousers. I will wear black and navy trousers but it will be slightly different. I think it looks too bland sometimes and I don't want this game to be bland. It's a fantastic game we play. It's a stylish game.'

During the first round of the 2009 Open at Turnberry, the British golfer wore a Union Jack waistcoat and red tartan trousers. It may have been intended as a patriotic gesture but it did little to inspire his game. After struggling in the blustery wind and rain on the second day, Poulter missed the cut by a considerable margin, finishing on a 14-over-par total of 154.

Afterwards he joked, 'I could have had a set of spades in my bag and I still wouldn't have found the middle of the fairway.'

In his two rounds Poulter managed to make only one birdie, prompting an ironic fist-pumping celebration at the 17th hole on the second day.

As he said later, 'You can only laugh!'

Robert Sommers:

During a practice round leading up to the 1988 Open, Jack Nicklaus tossed three balls into a bunker beside the 15th green at Royal Lytham and St Annes. He holed the first ball, and for an encore holed the second. He picked up the third.

When someone called, 'Why didn't you try the third?' he grinned and answered, 'You've got to be kidding!'

Barry Johnston:

Surprisingly, Seve Ballesteros never won a major when one of his three older brothers, Baldomero, Manuel and Vicente, was carrying his clubs. During the 1986 Masters it was Vicente who was caddie and Seve was leading the tournament by two strokes in the final round after he holed an eagle putt on the 13th. He embraced his brother Vicente in an emotional celebration and sportswriters began composing their Ballesteros victory stories. But they had hugged too soon. Two holes later Seve mishit a simple four-iron approach to the 15th green into the water, allowing Jack Nicklaus to put on the winner's green jacket for a record sixth time.

Four months later Vicente was again Seve's caddie at the 1986 Open at Turnberry. Before the start of the championship Ballesteros was the odds-on favourite to lift the claret jug for a third time, but the weather conspired against him. On the opening day a westerly wind gusting up to thirty-five miles an hour caused Seve to card a 6-over-par 76 for the first round.

After yet another shot ended up in the heavy, impenetrable rough, Vicente apologised to his brother for giving him the wrong club.

'It's not your fault,' said Seve, with a sigh. 'It's my fault because I listen to you!'

Nick Faldo:

Willie Aitcheson was perhaps the most famous caddie in professional golf during his highly successful partnership with Lee Trevino. Lee once told me a wonderful story about how he first came to work with Willie before he won the 1971 Open at Royal Birkdale, having sacked his original caddie after nine holes of practice:

So Willie joined me at the 10th and we marched down the fairway to my ball.

'How far is it to the pin?'

'Five-iron, surrr,' announced this Scottish voice at my side.

'I didn't ask you that, I asked you how far it is to the pin.'

'Disnae matter whit ye asked, it's still a five-iron, surrr.'

'How ... far ... is ... it ... to ... the ... pin?' I repeated a third time before reaching into my bag and pulling out five balls. I then hit a wedge, a seven-iron, a three-wood, a three-iron and a putter straight onto the green. So I looked at Willie and said, 'Don't ever tell me what club it is. Just give me the yardage!'

RYDER CUP

Ian Woosnam:

In most golf tournaments, the pressure builds up through four days and reaches a crescendo over the last nine holes on a Sunday afternoon. A Ryder Cup is different because that kind of gut-twisting pressure starts on the 1st tee on Day One and stays there until one team walks away with the small, gold trophy.

My first Ryder Cup was at Palm Beach Gardens, Florida, in 1983, and I was delighted to have been included, second only to Paul Way as the youngest member of the European team. As I hovered around the edges, we managed to win two of the four morning foursomes and eat lunch at 2–2. By then, I knew Sam Torrance and I would be playing Ben Crenshaw and Calvin Peete in what was the final four-ball match of the afternoon.

Sam has always been a good friend and he certainly

knew me well enough to notice I was incredibly tense on the 1st tee. In fact, at one stage, I thought I was going to be sick. I had always thought of myself as an easygoing type, but this kind of pressure was new.

'OK, Woosie, calm down now,' the Scot told me in his calmest, gentlest voice. 'Just take your time. I'll look after things for a few holes, just until you find your feet.'

'Thanks, I appreciate that.'

Sam sounded reassuring, and I was starting to feel better as he stepped onto the 1st tee. He placed his ball and proceeded to slice his drive way right. It landed out of bounds. He turned to look at me with an apologetic shrug of the shoulders and, in his broad Scottish accent, said: 'Welcome to the Ryder Cup, Woos!'

Sandy Lyle:

Brian Barnes, a Scot and a larger-than-life character, found celebrity by beating Jack Nicklaus twice in the same day during the 1975 Ryder Cup at Laurel Valley, with the assistance of US non-playing captain Arnold Palmer. The mischievous Palmer, who was forever trying to put one over on Nicklaus, the youthful upstart who had so ruthlessly swiped his crown as the king of golf, approached opposing skipper Bernard Hunt on the final morning of the first of two rounds of singles, to enquire if he might 'have anyone who can give Jack a game?'

The richly talented Brian Barnes, who might have become a serial major winner but for his tragic battle with alcohol, was nominated as the sacrificial offering, only to reject the role with a stunning 4 and 2 upset. Delighted with the success of his scheme, Palmer sidled up to Hunt during lunch to suggest, 'You know, I think if Brian were drawn against Jack this afternoon, he could beat him again . . .' After much nudge-nudge wink-wink verbal jousting, Hunt let slip that he was of a mind to name Barnes in the last match, which, by a massive coincidence (not!), was precisely the role Palmer had planned for his buddy.

As Brian delights in recalling at every available opportunity, when they renewed their acquaintance on the 1st tee, Nicklaus turned his ice-blue eyes, which could burn into an opponent's soul like a laser, on his earlier conqueror and said, 'Well done this morning, Barnsie, but there ain't no way you're going to beat me twice in one day . . .'

Brian triumphed again, this time 2 and 1, a result that Palmer could not resist mentioning in his victory speech: 'My thanks to the American team who did an outstanding job – even if Jack did lose two matches today to Brian Barnes. He doesn't mind really . . .'

At which point Nicklaus interjected, 'Oh yes I do!'

Barry Johnston:

When the American Ryder Cup player Tommy 'Thunder' Bolt was angry, no one was spared. Not even God. After missing a short putt one day, Bolt hollered up at the sky, 'Why don't you come down here and play me? Come on, come on. You and your kid too. I'll give you two a side and play your low ball!'

Bolt was renowned for hurling away his clubs if he was unhappy with a particular shot but sometimes even that was not enough. He once asked an official, 'I know you can be fined for throwing a club, but I want to know if you can be fined for throwing a caddie!'

Lawrence Donegan: Quiet Please

It was the final day of the 2002 Ryder Cup at The Belfry. Match one was due off at quarter past eleven. At 11.05, Colin Montgomerie and Sam Torrance strode purposefully down the steps leading from the practice putting green to the tee. Torrance had his hand on his player's shoulder. He was wearing the kind of smile fathers reserve for the day they escort their daughter down the aisle. The happy couple were followed a couple of minutes later by a grim Curtis Strange and a morose Scott Hoch.

Hoch has a reputation as a world-class whiner, so his hunched shoulders and sour expression came as no surprise. Less well known is that Montgomerie has never been Hoch's greatest fan. It started back at the 1997 Ryder Cup when the two played each other in what turned out to be a poisonous singles match. Back then Montgomerie had been denied a win because Seve Ballesteros, elated that the Cup had been secured, conceded a thirty-foot putt to the American. Maybe I was reading too much into a simple handshake but from where I was standing it looked like the two players wanted to wrestle rather than play 18 holes.

Photographs were taken, announcements made, last-minute instructions whispered in the ear. 'If he's got a putt to win the match, attack him with the three-wood,' I imagined Sam Torrance telling his man.

'On the tee ... Colin Montgomerie,' declared Ivor Robson, the suave, silver-haired starter.

It's long been my view that truly great golf shots should be judged on context. For instance, I have actually had a hole in one. Was it a great golf shot? Of course not. I was playing on my own on a wet Tuesday in Donegal and I was 26-over-par at the time. No one was there to see it, apart from me. Indeed, as the years have passed the more I have begun to think the entire episode might have been a dream.

By contrast, Colin Montgomerie's tee shot was a truly great golf shot. It was the first shot on the most important day of the greatest golf tournament in the world. He was surrounded by thousands of people. Millions of people were watching him on television. In the circumstances, I would have been expecting a round of applause if I'd demonstrated the ability to stand up straight. Montgomerie not only stood up straight, he hit a three-wood 300 yards down the left side of the fairway. If he'd rented a car, filled the tank full of rocket fuel and brought along an Ordnance Survey map of the West Midlands he couldn't have sent the ball any farther or placed it in a better spot.

As soon as Montgomerie stepped to the side of the tee, taking extra care not to follow the flight of the ball, I knew it was a guaranteed point to Europe. I'm equally certain Scott Hoch knew this too, which is why he semi-duffed his tee shot about eighty yards short of his opponent's.

The next match, between Sergio Garcia and David Toms, had just teed off when there was a huge roar from the 1st green. Either Montgomerie had holed a birdie putt to go one up or Scott Hoch had fallen backwards into a bunker. The news floated back: Montgomerie had holed a putt.

Clearly, Curtis Strange had noticed Torrance's fatherly approach to escorting his players to the tee and injected a bit more warmth into his entrances. David Toms got the arm around the shoulder treatment from his captain. Hal Sutton did too, then David Duval. At one stage I thought Strange was going to give Mark Calcavecchia a French kiss to help him on his way. Torrance responded by ratcheting up the proud father quotient. Big smiles, warmer hugs, fonder goodbyes.

By the time match eleven, between Phillip Price and Phil Mickelson, was due up on the tee, I was beginning to think I was at one of those Moonie ceremonies where hundreds of brides are led up the aisle to get married!

Barry Johnston:

One of the most memorable images of the 2008 Ryder Cup, at the Valhalla Golf Club in Louisville, Kentucky, was that of Boo Weekley in the Sunday singles matches.

After driving off from the 1st tee, the thirty-five-year-old outdoorsman from Florida stuck his driver between his legs, slapped his behind and galloped off down the fairway like a cowboy on a horse. He said, 'I felt like I just had to do it to loosen it up a little bit. I mean, it's just my nature to be a little goofy anyway!'

Weekley certainly loosened up the crowd, who chanted 'Boo-Sa! Boo-Sa!' every time he made a big putt or won a hole. He went on to win his match 4 and 2 against Oliver Wilson and his antics helped to inspire the American team to victory by a resounding 16½–11½, their biggest winning margin since 1981.

It was Boo Weekley's debut in the Ryder Cup and on the second day he described how the adrenalin from playing in such a major event was affecting him. He said, 'I feel like a dog that somebody done stuck a needle to and it juiced me up, like I've been running around a greyhound track chasing one of them bunnies.'

After his victory on the Sunday, Weekley was asked what the rabbit tasted like, now that he'd caught up with it.

He replied, 'Chicken!'

Barry Johnston:

The European victory in the 1987 Ryder Cup at Muirfield Village in Columbus, Ohio, was probably their most important in the history of the competition. It was the first time in sixty years that an American team had been beaten on their own soil. To add insult to injury, the course had been designed by the United States captain, Jack Nicklaus.

After Seve Ballesteros had sealed their momentous 15–13 victory by beating Curtis Strange, the jubilant European players danced all over the 18th green, led by José Maria Olazábal performing the cha-cha. The European captain, Tony Jacklin, apologised for his team's behaviour to Jack Nicklaus, who said ruefully, 'Don't worry about it. The way we played this week, I think I'll dig it up!'

Barry Johnston:

Paul Azinger is one of the most outspoken players to have featured in the Ryder Cup in recent years. At The Belfry in 1989 he played Seve Ballesteros in the singles and they accused each other of cheating. Azinger refused to let Ballesteros change a ball when the Spaniard claimed it was damaged. As payback, Ballesteros accused Azinger, who eventually won, of taking an illegal drop on the last hole. Two years later at Kiawah Island in South Carolina, in a Ryder Cup that became known as 'The War by the Shore', the feud between Azinger and Ballesteros escalated.

On the opening morning, Ballesteros and José Maria Olazábal accused Azinger and his partner Chip Beck of breaking the rules by changing their type of ball on the 7th tee. The Americans had to admit they were in the wrong. Azinger said, 'We made a mistake but we certainly weren't cheating.' Ballesteros smiled and patted Azinger on the shoulder. 'We don't say that. There's cheating and there's breaking the rules.' This so infuriated the Americans that they lost three of the next four holes and Ballesteros clinched the match with a birdie at the 18th.

Of course, when it came to stretching the rules, Ballesteros was not exactly innocent. He had a habit of developing an awkward cough, usually during his opponent's backswing, and was well known for distracting other players by standing in their line of vision as they putted. After the match Azinger referred to Ballesteros as 'The King of Gamesmanship'.

Seve Ballesteros remarked, 'The American team is made up of eleven gentlemen . . . and Paul Azinger!'

Barry Johnston:

The 1981 Ryder Cup at Walton Heath was won by the United States by a record score of 18½–9½ points. It remains the heaviest defeat that the European team has suffered at the hands of the Americans. By the end of the second day Europe were already down 10½–5½. On the final morning, Sam Torrance was due to play Lee

130

Trevino in the first of the singles matches and he offered to give Trevino a lift to the course in his car.

Once they had set off, Torrance joked with Trevino that he was going to drive them to London, so that if neither of them turned up, he would still get a half-point!

It might have been a good idea if he had.

Trevino beat him 5 and 3.

Ian Woosnam:

The 1987 Ryder Cup was held at Muirfield Village, near Dublin, Ohio. The European team captain Tony Jacklin sent Nick Faldo and me out third on the Friday morning, drawn to play foursomes against the formidable American pair of Masters champion Larry Mize and the aggressive Lanny Wadkins, and our status as the European 'dream team' wasn't looking too clever when we were three down after only 10 holes. We weren't exactly panicking, but the captain was following our match and he wasn't looking too thrilled.

We arrived at the 11th tee, and I was preparing to drive when the usual calm was interrupted by a large, middle-aged, square-jawed, brightly clothed American sitting at the back of the tee.

'Oh my!' he exclaimed, loud enough for everyone to hear. 'He's only a boy!'

I sensed a barely suppressed snigger in the gallery, but I focused on the back of the ball and thumped a drive straight down the fairway, where it finished forty yards past Mize's ball.

'Yes,' I declared as I bent to collect the tee peg, 'but think what I'll be like when I grow up and become a man!'

Barry Johnston:

A reporter once asked the 1999 European Ryder Cup captain, Mark James, why he walked around a golf course with his head down, looking as though he had just trodden in something rather unpleasant.

James replied, 'Because I grew up on a course with three thousand sheep on it!'

Barry Johnston:

After the first two days of the 1983 Ryder Cup match at the PGA National in Palm Beach Gardens, Florida, the teams were tied on eight points each. The United States had not lost on home soil since the Ryder Cup began in 1927 and before the all-important singles matches on Sunday their captain, Jack Nicklaus, informed his players bluntly, 'I will not be the first captain to blow this thing. Now you guys show me some brass!'

Fuzzy Zoeller was suffering from a bad back, so he was shocked to learn that he had been put up against Seve Ballesteros in the first match of the day. After 11 holes Ballesteros was three up, but Zoeller won the next four holes with two birdies and two pars and managed to halve the match. His half-point proved to be vital in the American team's narrow victory by 14½–13½.

After the match, Fuzzy Zoeller confessed, 'When Jack told me last night I had to play Seve, I took so many pills, I'm glad they don't have drug tests for golfers!'

Sam Torrance:

The first drama of the 2002 Ryder Cup at The Belfry came on the evening of the welcome dinner, as I was preparing to make my first speech as captain of the European team. My wife Suzanne, who had lived with my phobia about public speaking for three years, was spoiling me. She ran a bath and poured a glass of champagne for me to have in between the evening press conference and the dinner. She was getting her hair done.

It was about 6.30 p.m. I had been soaking and sipping for two minutes when the telephone rang.

'Hi Sam, it's Pierre here,' a Swedish accent said.

'Hi Pierre, what's up?'

'I've got a problem.'

'Yeah, what's wrong?'

'I can't tell you on the phone. It's the biggest problem of the week. I need to see you right away.'

'Okay, come on round,' I said.

As it happened, Pierre Fulke was in the room next to us and he was at the door in twenty seconds. So I jumped out of the bath, put a towel round me and answered the knock at the door. There he was, looking a bit ashen-faced.

'What the hell is wrong?' I asked.

Whereupon he brought his tie from behind his back and said, 'I can't do my tie!'

THE LADIES' TEE

Barry Johnston:

While she was still an amateur, Jenny Lee Smith won the inaugural Women's British Open Championship at Fulford in 1976. Five years later she was playing in the fourth round of the championship at the Northumberland Golf Club, in Gosforth Park, when she shanked her tee shot at the short 11th. Her ball flew way off to the right of the green and deposited itself in some tufty grass. As Jenny prepared to take her second shot she moved her right foot and was terrified to hear a high-pitched squeal. Her spiked shoe had trodden on a baby rabbit hiding in the long grass.

Fortunately, the rabbit was not badly injured and it scampered quickly away but Jenny's nerves were shattered. Badly shaken, she managed to finish the round and made it back to the clubhouse, where she gratefully accepted the offer of a cold, refreshing lager. But this was not to be her day.

As she tilted the glass in anticipation of the amber nectar, her hands still trembling, she did not notice a wasp lurking on the rim of the glass.

It stung her on the nose!

Nick Faldo:

When Fanny Sunesson became my caddie in 1990 we arranged to meet up at David Leadbetter's new training camp at Lake Nona, Florida. She reported for work on the first morning, typically bright-eyed and bushy-tailed.

'I appreciate it's not part of your normal duties, Fanny,' I greeted her, 'but I've forgotten to pack a toothbrush. Do you think you could nip back to the hotel and buy me a new one?' Ever attentive to detail, Fanny arrived back brandishing a choice of two toothbrushes.

'I do not know whether you wanted the hard bristols or the soft bristols,' she explained in that melodic Swedish singsong accent.

I gestured with cupped hands in front of my chest, 'No, Fanny, *these* are Bristols.'

Quick as a flash, Fanny shot back, 'Well, you don't want the soft ones then!'

Barry Johnston:

The first woman to wear trousers in a golf competition was a young player called Gloria Minoprio. Twenty-six-year-old Miss Minoprio caused a sensation at the British Ladies' Amateur Championship at Westward Ho! in October 1933 when she arrived for her first round at the north Devon golf club in a chauffeur-driven, yellow Rolls-Royce. She raised more eyebrows when she stepped out of the car carrying just one club, the straight-faced iron known as a cleek.

But what outraged the officials of the Ladies' Golf Union, and delighted the throng of spectators, was her outfit. At that time the standard attire for a lady golfer was a sensible skirt, sleeved upper clothing, and a hat or bandeau. The tall, dark-haired Miss Minoprio was wearing a turban-like woollen black cap, a high-necked, close-fitting white sweater, white kid gloves and a pair of figure-hugging midnight blue trousers.

Her outfit was deemed to be scandalous and improper but there was nothing in the rules to prevent it. The LGU promptly issued a statement deploring anyone who 'departs from the proper decorous costume of the traditional lady golfer'. Gloria played the round with her single club and, perhaps inevitably, struggled to compete on the seaside links and lost, but a clearly smitten Henry Longhurst wrote that she would 'go down to posterity with an immortality that is denied to kings and bishops, generals and statesmen, as "the lady who played in trousers"'.

Undeterred, Gloria Minoprio returned to the Ladies' Championship the following year at Seacroft, near Skegness, still with her one club. This time she won on the Monday, only to lose the next day, prompting Longhurst to write: 'Sic Transit Gloria Tuesday!'

Barry Johnston:

When Peter Dobereiner was at a golf club in Melbourne, he enquired whether they had women members. He was told, 'No, why do you ask?' Dobereiner explained that he had just seen two women putting on the 18th green outside the bar window.

'Oh,' sniffed the club official dismissively, 'they're not women members. They are associates!'

Tim Brooke-Taylor:
THE THREE BEARS

Once upon a time there were three bears who lived together in a house of their own; one of these was called Little Bear, and one was called Mummy Bear, and the other was called Golden Bear. And they each had a full set of irons, and they each had a pro-links golf trolley, and they each had a membership subscription for the local golf club, and they each played off a 10 handicap.

And one day, after they had gone out to pick up their copy of *Golfing World*, a little girl called Goldilocks passed by the house and looked in at the window, and seeing nobody in the house she lifted the latch and went in. When she saw three sets of golf clubs she first tried the seven-iron of Golden Bear, but it was too stiff; then she tried the four-iron of Mummy Bear, but it was too whippy; then she tried the three-iron of Little Bear, and it was just perfect.

And then she looked around and saw three golf trolleys in a little line. So she tried the first one belonging to Golden Bear but it was too heavy and she could hardly move it; then she tried the second one belonging to Mummy Bear, but that wasn't quite right either; and then finally she tried the one belonging to Little Bear and it was very easy to control and just what she was looking for.

And then, because she was a nosy little sod, she decided to go upstairs, where she found a massive wardrobe full of golfing gear. She decided to try on the gear belonging to Golden Bear, but it was really loud and screamed back at her from the mirror and made her look like Coco the Clown on an acid trip. Then she tried the golfing gear of Mummy Bear, but female golfers have never quite got it together fashionwise have they? And, oh God, look at those awful slacks! And then she tried on the golfing gear of Little Bear and it was just what she was looking for, and to cut a long story short, the three bears returned home half an hour later and managed to sell her a matched set of golf clubs, and several golfing pullovers, and a new golfing umbrella, and six pairs of golfing shoes and a new golf trolley (even though she'd bought a brand new one only two weeks ago), and over two thousand pounds' worth of golfing accessories, and . . .

And the moral of the story is: never let yourself get tricked into looking round an empty club shop when the pro isn't there, because you're bound to end up spending a fortune!

Barry Johnston:

Vivien Saunders was the first European woman to qualify for the US LPGA Tour and won the Women's British Open in 1977. She was a pioneer of women's rights in golf and often came face to face with male prejudice early in her career. For example, when she joined the Professional Golfers Association in 1969, there was a rule that stated, 'Lady members shall have the same rights as men, save they may not attend meetings, play in tournaments or vote.'

On one occasion when Vivien missed a vital putt during a championship, she cried out, 'Knickers!' and was rebuked by tournament officials.

Later in the round she changed her exclamation to 'Bee's knees!' – and was still told off!

Barry Johnston:

The Australian golfer Jan Stephenson won three majors on the LPGA Tour in the early 1980s but she became almost as famous for her sex-appeal as her golf. The glamorous blonde from Sydney posed naked in a bathtub full of golf balls and even had her own pin-up calendar. So she was considered to be something of an expert when *Golf Magazine* published a centrefold featuring male PGA Tour golfers.

After inspecting the photograph closely, Jan observed, 'Well, it just goes to show what we've been saying all along. That all the good-looking golfers are on the ladies' tour!'

Robert Sommers:

Among the most exclusive of British clubs, Royal St George's has a decidedly male flavour. At one time the club displayed a sign declaring, 'No dogs; no women.'

Times change; women won gradual recognition, but still St George's would have its way. A later sign, while acknowledging women were welcome in the clubhouse, proclaimed:

'Ladies wearing trousers are requested to remove them before entering the clubhouse!'

Barry Johnston:

Nancy Lopez was the most popular golfer of her generation. She dominated women's golf in the late 1970s and 1980s, after bursting onto the golf scene at the age of

WITH ACKNOWLEDGEMENTS TO
H. M. BATEMAN

twenty-one. In 1978 she won five consecutive tournaments and became the only player to win the Rookie of the Year Award, the Player of the Year Award and the Vare Trophy all in the same season. She went on to win the LPGA Championship three times.

Nancy's vibrant and outgoing personality swiftly endeared her to golf fans and helped to raise the profile of the women's game around the world. On one occasion she was playing in a tournament at Springfield, Illinois, when her playing partner needed to make a forty-foot putt to win the hole. As the ball set off across the green, Dee Darden, who was Lopez's caddie for five years, turned to Nancy and muttered, 'You watch this – she'll probably knock it in!'

The ball rolled right up to the hole but then it stopped suddenly a few inches short. The other player was distraught. More than that, she was furious. She exclaimed bitterly, 'I can't ever get a break! That should have gone in the hole! It was in all the way!' As she carried on and on, Dee Darden turned again to Lopez and quipped, 'You know if it was raining soup, she'd be out there with a fork!'

Nancy still had to make her own four-footer, but she could not stop herself laughing. Turning her back so the other player would not see, she chuckled to her caddie, 'Dee, if you ever say something like that to me again, I'm going to hit you right in the head!'

P.G. Wodehouse: *Tangled Hearts*

Agnes Flack measured her distance. She waggled. Slowly and forcefully she swung back. And her club was just descending in a perfect arc, when Smallwood Bessemer spoke.

'Hey!' he said.

In the tense silence the word rang out like the crack of a gun. It affected Agnes Flack visibly. For the first time since she had been a slip of a child, she lifted her head in the middle of a stroke, and the ball, badly topped, trickled over the turf, gathered momentum as it reached the edge of the tee, bounded towards the water, hesitated on the brink for an instant like a timid diver on a cold morning and then plunged in.

'Too bad,' said Julia Prebble.

Agnes Flack did not reply. She was breathing heavily through her nostrils. She turned to Smallwood Bessemer.

'You were saying something?' she asked.

'I was only going to remind you to relax,' said Smallwood Bessemer. 'Alex Morrison lays great stress on the importance of pointing the chin and rolling the feet. To my mind, however, the whole secret of golf consists in relaxing. At the top of the swing the muscles should be . . . '

'My niblick, please,' said Agnes Flack to her caddie.

She took the club, poised it for an instant as if judging

its heft, then began to move forward swiftly and stealthily, like a tigress of the jungle.

Until that moment, I had always looked on Smallwood Bessemer as purely the man of intellect, what you would describe as the thoughtful, reflective type. But he now showed that he could, if the occasion demanded it, be the man of action. I do not think I have ever seen anything move quicker than the manner in which he dived head-foremost into the thick clump of bushes which borders the 18th tee. One moment, he was there; the next, he had vanished. Eels could have taken his correspondence course.

It was a move of the highest strategic quality. Strong woman though Agnes Flack was, she was afraid of spiders!

Barry Johnston:

In 1983 Canadian amateur golfer Elaine Johnson was amazed when her shot struck a tree, ricocheted backwards, and the ball landed in her bra.

She exclaimed, 'I'll take the two-stroke penalty, but I'll be damned if I'll play the ball where it lays!'

Barry Johnston:

Dinah Oxley was a member of the Great Britain and Ireland Curtis Cup teams of 1968, 1970, 1972 and 1976.

The most significant shot of her career, however, took place during a practice round before the 1971 British Ladies' Amateur Golf Championship at Alwoodley, near Leeds.

Miss Oxley sliced a drive so wildly that the ball went flying out of bounds and onto a nearby road, where it shattered the windscreen of a car being driven by James Henson, an airline pilot.

Although badly shaken by the incident, Henson, who flew with BOAC (British Overseas Airways Corporation, later to become part of British Airways), kept calm and managed to pull his car safely to the side of the road. A distraught Miss Oxley ran out to check that the driver was not badly injured. When she saw that James Henson was unhurt, she invited him to wait in the Alwoodley clubhouse while his windscreen was being repaired.

The attractive lady golfer and the dashing airline pilot began talking in the club bar. They got on very well together. In fact, they got on so well, the next time she played in the Curtis Cup, her name was Dinah Oxley Henson!

Michael Parkinson:

'The magic's gone,' said the wife.

'If this is the parting of the ways, can I have custody of the *Wisdens*?'

'I'm not talking about our marriage, you twerp. The magic has gone from my golf,' she said.

I said I was relieved, although it didn't take me long to work out that a divorce would be considerably cheaper than my wife's continued search for perfection on the golf course. She has propped up the economy of several countries by her generous and dedicated support of local golf professionals, and throughout the world there are teachers and caddies whose eyes light up when they hear Mrs Parkinson is on the way to pay a visit.

It is sad when someone who has such dedication and love for golf becomes depressed by it. So when the wife announced that the magic had departed her game, I broke the rule of a lifetime and said I would play a round of winter golf. My attitude to winter golf is cautious. I see no sense in dressing up like a lighthouse keeper to play a round of golf, but clearly the crisis in my wife's life took precedence over my ambition never to be cold on a golf course again.

So off we went to regain the magic. I teed off, walked over to my wife on the ladies' tee and together we strolled down the 1st. I found my ball and was surprised I couldn't see the wife's ball on the fairway since the last time she missed the cut stuff, Jim Callaghan was the Prime Minister. We searched for her ball, she moaning all the while that this was certain proof the magic had gone forever and me nearly believing her.

We were joined by two greenkeepers and then by a friendly four-ball making their way back to the club-house. There were now eight of us engaged in trying to find the wife's ball. We must have looked like a line of volunteers helping the police in an inch-by-inch search for clues.

Finally, I said to her, 'Think back to the tee. What sort of shot did you play? Did you hit it well?'

The search stopped as she pondered the question. Our future strategy depended upon her reply.

'Oh, my God,' she said.

'What is it?' I cried.

'I didn't hit the ball at all,' she said.

'You missed it?' I said.

'No, I forgot to take the drive,' she said.

Later, in the clubhouse, the general consensus was that they had never heard anything like it. We could all tell stories of drives that ended up in trees, or down a rabbit hole, or in the back of a passing lorry. But none of us could recall an instance when the player forgot to take a shot.

It has to be reported that the wife made light of her forgetfulness. By the time we reached the 16th I was three down with three to play, which is the way it has always been and no doubt ever will be. She won the game on the 18th by chipping in for a birdie.

'Magic,' I said. She gave me an old-fashioned look.

149

Providing she remembers in future to take every shot, I can see little wrong with her game. Mind you, I'm the last person you should ask about magic.

If you've never had it, how do you know what you're looking for?!

THE RULES OF GOLF

Patrick Campbell:

Excluding the nine Rules of Etiquette and in Section II the thirty-four 'Definitions', there are forty-one Rules of Play, nearly all of which have about half a dozen sub-sections, and with the possible exception of Rule I – 'The Game of Golf consists in playing a ball from the teeing ground into the hole by successive strokes in accordance with the Rules' – all of them are lively provokers of strife.

For this reason the expert player prefers to leave them strictly alone, an abstinence assisted by his almost total ignorance of their content.

Up till 1 January 1960, a few class men could give you a rough quote of some of the better known ones, but then the Royal and Ancient amended them and pretty well everyone gave up.

Golf, in fact, is the only game in the world in which a precise knowledge of the rules can earn one a reputation for bad sportsmanship!

Barry Johnston:

When Hawaiian prodigy Michelle Wie reached sixteen in October 2005, she announced that she was turning professional and promptly signed sponsorship contracts with Nike and Sony reputed to be worth $10 million a year.

However, in her first professional event at the 2005 Samsung World Championship in Palm Desert, Wie was disqualified from a fourth-place finish after signing an incorrect scorecard. Then in the 2006 Women's British Open at Royal Lytham she finished tied-26th but was given a two-stroke penalty for grounding her club in a bunker at the 14th. The teenager admitted that she was not familiar with the rules.

'There was a piece of moss right behind my ball,' Wie told journalists later. 'I thought if you hit dirt it would be OK but I guess I knew the rule wrong. So it's a good learning experience. But I'm only sixteen.'

She was asked whether she planned to read *The Rules of Golf*, now that she had been penalised twice in less than a year.

She smiled apologetically and said, 'Well, they're not actually great reading material!'

Robert Sommers:

President Eisenhower took occasional licence with the rules of golf. During his presidency he played Burning Tree Club every Wednesday he could, quickly becoming known for his novel method of identifying his ball. Rather than stoop over for a closer look, he would use a club and roll his ball over until the trademark became visible. If his ball moved into a better lie, well, Ike *was* the President.

One afternoon Eisenhower's ball settled in the rough. When he tried to roll it over, it lodged against a rock. Startled, the President glared at his caddie and snapped, 'What happened?'

The caddie answered, 'Mr President, I'm afraid you have over-identified your ball!'

Peter Alliss:

Due to the homogenised state we now live in, everybody in the world of sport, due to the various trials by television, has to be whiter than white, purer than pure. Not so that great American professional Tommy Bolt, as good a ball striker as the world has ever seen. Yes, he was that good, winner of the 1958 US Open. And to say the least, he was one of *the* characters of the day. Why? Well, he used to throw the odd club, use an expletive or two and had a walk that wouldn't have disgraced a sheriff walking down the main street of some Texas town 125 years ago.

Tommy disliked the college kids. It was all too new. Youngsters with modest talent were offered golf scholarships at universities. Some probably played more golf than the pros and perhaps still do to this day. They would finish their studies and then attack the world of professional golf with relish. He always said they had an awful lot to learn, they didn't even know how to throw clubs properly. Some of them were stupid enough to throw them *backwards* so someone had to go back and retrieve them.

It was about this time the PGA introduced a rule whereby you could only hit a maximum of two shots onto a green during a practice round. The reason? Well, for years players, particularly those who took the game seriously, would pepper the greens with five or six shots until they got the feel of the shot. On this occasion Tommy hit three, or maybe four, onto a green. An official rushed out, 'Tommy, Tommy, I'm sorry, we've got to fine you, you know the rule, you can only hit two, so far you've hit seven extra shots during the round and this is only the twelfth.'

Tommy, who always carried a wad of cash, pulled out a roll of hundred dollar bills and gave him a couple saying airily, 'Keep the change, I may hit a couple more!'

Michael Green: The Art of Coarse Golf

The secret of successful Coarse Golf is to arouse emotion in the opponent. Sympathy is one of the best emotions, because once an opponent feels it would be unfair if he won the game, the battle is half over.

Askew's normal way of achieving this is to fall into a deep reverie while addressing the ball and to stare fixedly at the ground.

He then heaves a sigh, comes to with a start, and says, 'I'm sorry about that, old chap. I was just thinking how in the midst of life we are in death, as the Good Book has it.'

He gives no further explanation except perhaps to say what the Good Book is, if an opponent should think he means the Rules of Golf.

Another of his ingenious alternatives is to add, 'Funny how one gets attached to animals, isn't it? I mean they twine their little paws around your heart with their funny ways. You know, I can see him standing there now with his tail wagging and those trusting eyes looking up at me. I should never have let him off the lead. Ah well, better get on with the game I suppose. Life is for the living.'

This actually reduced one opponent to tears.

'Keep thinking of that little dog of yours,' he said apologetically, wiping his eyes. 'I had one like that. Then one day we left the front gate open and he ran away. But the wife always leaves the gate open for him to come back. We know that one day we'll hear his little paws pattering up the path.'

Unfortunately, this sad story so affected Askew that the round had to be abandoned, as both players were blubbering into their handkerchiefs.

Robert Sommers:

During the Battle of Britain in the Second World War, the St Mellons Golf and Country Club, in Monmouthshire, adopted a set of unusual rules for unusual circumstances. Written by G.L. Edsell, the club secretary, they read:

(1) Players are asked to collect the bomb and shrapnel splinters to prevent their causing damage to the mowing machines.

(2) In competition, during gunfire or while bombs are falling, players may take shelter without penalty for ceasing play.

(3) The positions of known delayed-action bombs are marked by red flags at a reasonable but not guaranteed safe distance therefrom.

(4) Shrapnel and/or bomb splinters on the fairways or in bunkers within a club's length of a ball may be moved without penalty, and no penalty shall be incurred if a ball is therefore caused to move accidentally.

(5) A ball moved by enemy action may be replaced, or if lost or destroyed, a ball may be dropped without penalty, not nearer the hole.

(6) A ball lying in a crater may be lifted and dropped not nearer the hole, preserving the line to the hole, without penalty.

(7) A player whose stroke is affected by the simultaneous explosion of a bomb may play another ball under penalty of one stroke.

Peter Dobereiner:

These days golf is much more vigilant in enforcing the rules and monitoring standards of deportment and behaviour, which is just as well since a lapse into the unsporting ethic which is increasingly infecting other popular sports would leave us without a game to play. It is impossible for an angry man or a dishonest man to play golf properly, although some still try it on.

One competitor in a recent Open Championship was disqualified, and subsequently banned from professional golf for forty-five years. When the referee was asked by how much the player had been moving his marker on the green, he answered that it would have to be measured in fractions of a mile rather than fractions of a foot.

A Ryder Cup captain ordered his team not to help look for American balls in the rough and, when the players protested, he sheepishly sought to justify his unsporting command by saying he was afraid of penalties for accidentally moving an opponent's ball. (There is, of course, no penalty if you accidentally move an opponent's ball during a search.)

In a subsequent foursomes match, a player refused to help search for his own ball. He carved his approach shot deep into the jungle and then sat down on his golf bag and rested while his partner and their opponents went off to hunt for the ball.

The knowledge that your behaviour on the course is liable to be relayed to the TV screens in twenty million homes, including the one watched by your wife and children, is undoubtedly a restraining influence on today's players.

Some of the game's more colourful characters simply could not have played tournament golf in today's conditions. There was one who released his internal pressures of frustration and disgust by head-butting trees, kicking himself on the shins and, on one occasion, knocking himself out with a self-inflicted left hook. One of his contemporaries who was waiting to drive off was the target of some wounding verbal abuse from a spectator. The player turned his back on his tormentor, bent over and broke wind, effectively ending further discussion.

I had planned to offer a substantial cash reward from my personal fortune for the first reader to submit an all-correct list identifying the heroes of the above incidents. To my deep disappointment it has been officially deemed that any such competition would jeopardise the amateur status of everyone involved. That would never do.

Few of us can aspire to the level of moral rectitude of the lady captain of Effingham Golf Club, near London. Her four-ball was putting out when a naked flasher leapt out of the bushes. The lady captain fixed him with a laser stare and in tones of righteous outrage demanded, 'Are you a member?'

Tony Jacklin:

Tommy Bolt was a man I considered something of a tortured genius, and he could be wicked and profane at times. He was a devil. He had a habit of passing gas on the tee, and once he let go with a long and loud fart as a PGA official stood nearby.

'Do that again, Bolt, and I'm going to have to fine you,' said the official.

Bolt grumbled and said, 'That's the trouble with you guys, you're taking all the colour out of the game!'

Robert Sommers:

When the 1999 US Open came to Pinehurst, in North Carolina, tales of the old resort's past spun in every corner of the clubhouse, especially those about Richard S. Tufts, whose family not only created the resort but the entire village of Pinehurst before the turn of the twentieth century.

Aside from his position at Pinehurst, Tufts had been a major figure in golf administration, and an authority on the rules of the game. A man with a sense of humour, he liked to tell of the time he had been called onto the No. 2 course to make a ruling during a tournament. When he arrived at the site he found two golfers who'd had more than a few drinks sitting on the edge of a bunker. As he moved closer he asked the nature of the problem.

One spoke up and said, 'One of us is one-up, but we don't know which one of us it is.'

Tufts, the man who wrote many of the rules golfers play by, had no answer!

Peter Alliss:

Much has been made of the introduction in 2008 of drug testing for golfers, both men and women. I'm not quite sure how it's going to work. To my full knowledge no pill has been invented that makes you a better putter, one who never misses from four feet, or slices a drive away right out of bounds when the wind is blowing from left to right. But years ago, when the first serious campaigns began in an attempt to stop people smoking, many ideas were suggested to stop the craving.

A friend of mine from Bournemouth reported that his regular golfing partner had given up smoking and was living on Polo mints and his game was improving! So I was amused to get the following from:

R&A Committee (Rules)
Fox House
Glacier Street
Bournemouth

Subject: Investigation into the use of drugs as applied to mid-handicap, upper/lower quartile age group,

*golfers to identify the organic digestive bowelic inhib-
itive addictive sexualist effects thereof.*

Sir

*My Committee has instructed me to write to you re
the above – as it applies to yourself.*

*It has been brought to our attention that you are in
the habit – during actual play – of eating/sucking/
crunching a proprietary brand of mint commercially
sold as 'Polo'.*

*While this activity may on the surface appear to be
quite innocuous, I have to bring to your attention
the fact that as the aforementioned mint may contain
microscopic amounts of the substance dihexythe-
drylanicmexain, it can under certain conditions, viz.
before, during, after or instead of alcohol or sex – or
in moments of high emotional stress, e.g. 1st tee on
Sunday morning – be considered to be a drug within
the meaning of the Act.*

*Although legally speaking the intake of such artificial
aids does not at this moment contravene the R&A
Rules, such actions are not considered to be in the
best interests of the game.*

*Having read reports regarding your standard of play,
my Committee accepts that you are obviously in need*

of something to counteract the depressive nature of your normal game. However, whilst we have no statutory powers to order you to stop taking this power-driving, one-putting aid, we would urge you to:

(a) limit your intake to the hours of bunker play;
(b) resist the temptation to whistle through the centre hole whilst your opponent is on his backswing;
(c) at least hand the bloody things round.

I am, Sir, your obedient servant,
Ivor Trebor

PRO-CELEBRITY

Peter Alliss:

Some of us had arrived a day or two early at Gleneagles in readiness for the filming of *Pro-Celebrity Golf*. We had a rather good dinner together and decided that the very next day the eight of us would each put a tenner in the pot and play Stableford competition off handicap. Suffice to say, we stayed up rather late. This was the occasion I was introduced to a drink called a Rusty Nail, which slipped down very nicely indeed, but *wow* – you don't want too many of those to get the job done. We decided we'd go to bed but we did have a master plan just in case the weather was poor the next day. Whoever woke up first would ring round and let the others know the weather forecast and, if we decided that golf was out of the question, we'd rendezvous in the sauna.

I woke at about 6.30 a.m. with what sounded like airgun pellets hitting the window of my room. Now there are degrees of rain at the Gleneagles Hotel in Perthshire. Occasionally, there's a light mist that drifts down the glen and gets you a bit wet if you stay out in it too long. Then you have, what I was observing at the time, airgun pellets, which become shotgun pellets of the 12-bore variety, working up to 303 heavy calibre machine-gun fire. This one grew rapidly and by the time I got my head together and found out the room numbers of my companions, it was still belting down. I called round and we decided those who could would rendezvous in the sauna at about 8.30 a.m.

The sauna was quite large; it would seat eight or ten people comfortably. When I arrived Sean '007' Connery was perched in the corner stark naked, sitting on a small towel next to a tub of pine-scented water with a big wooden ladle in his hand, which he dipped into the beautiful liquid and then emptied over the hot coals. The immense cloud of steam that arose took one's breath away. It was red hot, but the smell was delicious. I arranged my small towel on the wooden slats and sat down. Suddenly I noticed, lying on the floor, the great jockey, Geoff Lewis.

'What are you doing down there?' I asked, which is a pretty silly question when you think of it. His reply was intriguing.

'Do you know,' he said, 'I must have had ten thousand saunas in my life. Heat rises, so if you want to stay in a long time, you lie on the floor. You still get very hot, you sweat, so you should drink something. I'm on my holidays, remember, so I bought a bottle of champagne, which contains no calories. So I'm just going to lie on the floor, and occasionally have a sip of champagne. I can tell you it does you the world of good.' I thought, I must try that.

Through the door came Jimmy Tarbuck, closely followed by Bruce Forsyth. They arranged their towels and Sean poured more water on the coals, creating even more steam and heat. Next to arrive was Kenny Lynch, singer/songwriter/comedian, an amusing cove and great side-kick of Mr Tarbuck. The heat was almost unbearable. Sweat was dripping off our bodies on to the poor, unfortunate Mr Lewis, who didn't seem to care a jot. There were one or two moans, the odd belch, then suddenly, through the glass door we saw Eric Sykes approaching.

Quick as a flash Tarbuck said, 'Here's Eric coming. Don't say anything when he arrives, everybody shush, not a word. Odds on he won't have his hearing aid in.'

Eric came through the door. Slipping out of his robe he arranged his towel and sat down. Now to say Eric was thin would be an understatement. His ribs looked like the deck of a stacked xylophone. He sat down, looked around and said, 'What a pity about this rain. I was so looking forward to playing today.' Silence, everyone looking straight ahead. Eric continued, 'You know what I've found playing here at Gleneagles, you really need a local caddie. You can go hopelessly wrong if you don't have someone who knows the line on the greens.' Nothing, just drip, drip, drip. The sweat continued to drop onto poor old Geoff.

Connery poured another spoonful of scented water on the coals, the heat rose, there were one or two more groans, again the odd belch, heads were held in hands and someone broke wind silently, there was a distinct aroma in the air. The scene was one of self-inflicted agony. Sean, as 007, was at the height of his fame. He stood up to rearrange his towel and his physique was quite magnificent. There was a good deal of observation of what the Americans call 'noble parts'. My wife had always had a crush on Sean and I was sorry she wasn't there because his noble parts were perhaps not much more noble than mine. But I digress.

Eric looked around at this strange scene, bodies of various shapes and skins of different hues dripping sweat, slight moaning and groaning, and uttered the immortal words, 'Can anyone tell me what time this train gets into Calcutta?'

Barry Johnston:

During the Bob Hope Classic in Palm Springs one year, Jimmy Tarbuck was partnering the 1976 US Open winner, Jerry Pate, when a deafening roar went up from the next hole. It turned out that Arnold Palmer had scored a hole in one in the first round. As they walked on, Pate and Tarbuck passed a golf steward who was still unaware of what had happened. He enquired irritably, 'What the hell was all that noise back there?'

Pate told him, 'Arnold Palmer's just had a hole in one.'

The bored official was less than impressed.

'Well, so he should. He plays often enough!'

Peter Alliss:

In one programme of *Pro-Celebrity Golf* I played in partnership with Ted Dexter against Ben Crenshaw and the Formula One world champion James Hunt, who came complete with Oscar, a magnificent Alsatian and quite the largest dog I've ever seen in my life, and the most beautifully behaved. He was never on a lead; only a thin collar with his boss's telephone number on it was needed to keep Oscar on the straight and narrow. He used to pad quietly behind his master, even into the great dining room. James would point, Oscar would sit like a statue, his eyes following his master as he made his way to his table, never taking his eyes off him until dinner was over.

Oscar also loved the golf course but he had a disconcerting habit of sitting with his nose about eighteen inches from the ball as it was about to be driven. As soon as the shot was on its way, Oscar would charge down the fairway in a great effort to see where it had gone. He never got more than seventy or eighty yards before returning but, for some, it was disconcerting, particularly when Oscar started to move before the club-head had reached the ball!

Barry Johnston:

Isao Aoki was the first Japanese golfer to achieve international success. He won the 1978 World Match Play

Championship at Wentworth and finished runner-up to Jack Nicklaus in the 1980 US Open. In his early days as a professional, Aoki did not speak very good English, and on one occasion he was playing with Eric Sykes in a pro-celebrity event at Fulford Heath in the West Midlands. After they had both driven from the 1st tee, the pair were walking up together, when Eric asked his Japanese partner, 'What did you think of my tee shot?'

Aoki thought for a moment and then stopped and bowed politely.

'Very good,' he said, 'but sleeves a little long!'

Bruce Forsyth:

I was the only person to play in every series of the *Pro-Celebrity Golf*. I think this was mainly because I always made myself available. There were too many wonderful moments to mention them all, but possibly the funniest was the day when both James Hunt and Peter Cook took part. James had this beautiful Alsatian, Oscar, who accompanied him around the course for his morning match. At every tee and every green, the dog would patiently sit to one side, then follow his master on to the next.

After lunch, Peter Cook was playing. He duly approached the 1st tee. As he did so, we noticed that he was carrying a goldfish in a bowl, which he set down beside his clubs.

'What's all this, Peter?' asked Peter Alliss.

'Well,' he said, 'James Hunt was allowed to bring his dog along with him. The only pet I've got is my goldfish, and he just loves to come along with me when I play.'

And come along it did. After every shot, Peter picked the bowl up and walked to where his ball had landed, put it down, played his shot, then picked it up again and took it to his next shot – for all 18 holes!

Michael Parkinson:

Playing in your first pro-celebrity golf match is a voyage into the unknown like marriage or eating haggis or entering a ferret legging competition for the first time. In other words, you start by anticipating the best and end up with a ferret in your underpants.

I speak from raw and bitter experience. When the invitation arrived to play four days in a pro-celebrity tournament on a championship course in the Home Counties, I should have thrown the letter in the fire. Instead, I accepted, giddy with the innocence of one new to the game.

Looking back, I should have retired after the very first day, nay even the first hole, because in truth it was blindingly obvious from the beginning that the entire enterprise was going to be a dreadful ordeal. At the 1st tee there were a good few hundred people to see us on

our way. My three playing partners went ahead of me and drove the ball up the fairway in the approved manner.

I chose an alternative method. Using my three-wood I contrived to hit the ball on its head so that it buried the tee and rolled forward all of six inches. The crowd stood in horrified silence, my playing partners shuffled uncomfortably like people who see a drunken friend try to shake hands with a hat stand.

The silence was cracked by my caddie who said in a stage whisper, 'Look on the bright side. It only went six inches but it was dead on target!'

During that first round and through the ensuing three days my caddie found my golf distinctly humorous. His lack of faith in my ability was obvious and at every tee shot when the other caddies would await their players' putt by positioning themselves 200 yards or so down the fairway, he would hide behind the nearest tree. This ploy did nothing for my confidence and caused mild panic among spectators who were quite rightly concerned that, if I terrified my caddie, I might do them a terrible mischief.

He was unremitting in his attitude. Once when I played an exquisite chip to within a foot of the flag, he dropped to the ground in a mock faint. Again, when I hit an eight-iron out of a bunker on to the green, a shot even my pro saluted, my caddie was unimpressed. As he handed me the putter, he said, 'You lucky sod.'

174

But the final comment was delivered by a young fan who approached me on the last day with her autograph book. She asked politely for my signature and then busied herself finding an appropriate page. She flicked over the section marked 'golf professionals', to which I could have no objection, but also passed through the section marked 'celebrities', which worried me slightly. In the end she found what she was looking for. My appropriate section. She handed me the book.

The page was headed 'miscellaneous'!

Alex Hay:

A very funny man with an insatiable appetite for golf is Jimmy Tarbuck. He plays a higher standard than many of his celebrated colleagues and travels everywhere to compete in the Pro-Am events that precede major tournaments, so helping to raise large sums for charity.

His first visit to Woburn was in fact the very first time television filming ever took place there. One of America's top players, Billy Casper, was making a series of instructional films and Jim and footballer Bobby Charlton were to be his guinea pigs.

The trio stood on the tee with Casper in the centre, his arms around the others' shoulders. He had just jetted in, but with true American professionalism he went smoothly into action as the cameras rolled.

'Hi folks! I'm Billy Casper and I wanna introduce you to a couple of very good friends of mine here at the beautiful WOBUCK Country Club. First Jimmy TARBURN.'

Jim's face never changed, not even a flicker. Casper went on, 'One of England's best-known entertainers. Welcome, Jimmy.'

Jim replied, 'I wanna say what a great thrill it is being here with you, Arnie.'

Casper's reaction was not quite so calm!

Barry Johnston:

King Baudouin of Belgium was a very keen golfer and played to a handicap of three. He had succeeded to the throne in 1951, at the age of twenty-one, after the abdication of his father, Leopold III, and he enjoyed playing golf with visiting celebrities and professionals. On one occasion he was paired with England's Ryder Cup captain Dai Rees in a pro-amateur tournament at Gleneagles – a partnership the local press gleefully described as 'The King and Dai.'

Bob Hope once played with King Baudouin against two top-ranked Belgian players and at one point the King turned to the comedian and remarked drily, 'You must have a lot of money, Mr Hope.'

Hope laughed and replied, 'I don't even own a country!'

When Ben Hogan was on holiday in Europe he was also invited to play a round of golf with the King of the Belgians. The old master was unimpressed. 'Sorry,' he said, 'I don't play golf while on vacation!'

Bruce Forsyth:

My most embarrassing moment was at Finchley Golf Club when I was playing with Brian Barnes. There had been a lot of rain so the ground was very soft. I had to play off a sloping fairway, but still thought I could play

a three-wood. The ball was below my feet. I took my stance and made a swing, which felt good. I then looked down the fairway, but Brian shouted, 'The ball's still there, Bruce!'

'Where?' I called back.

On further investigation, I found it buried deep in the turf, right by my feet. It had gone straight through the wet, soggy ground and been covered by the grass.

When he was asked to comment on my swing, Brian Barnes said, 'With a swing like that he'll always make a good dancer!'

US OPEN

Barry Johnston:

Lou Graham was the unlikely winner of the 1975 US Open at the Medinah Country Club in Illinois, after beating John Mahaffey by two strokes in an 18-hole playoff. It was only Graham's third win on the PGA Tour in eleven years. Afterwards one newspaper commented that the new US Open champion was so unknown, he was difficult to recognise.

Graham complained, 'Now that really chapped me off. My wife was madder than me. She said, "Honey, I recognise you every time I see you and the children recognise you half the time!"'

Peter Alliss:

The old firebrand Tommy Bolt was well known for throwing clubs and even breaking them over his knee. But a couple of times Tommy got his comeuppance. Once he was arguing with a caddie about which club to use for his approach to a green. Bolt thought it was a five-iron, the caddie insisted it was a six.

Tommy took out the five-iron and hit his ball twenty yards over the green. Furious, he snapped the five-iron over his knee. The caddie meanwhile, not too happy himself, promptly snapped the six-iron over his own knee, dropped Bolt's bag and walked off the course.

Another time, Bolt was playing well in the opening round of the US Open at Cherry Hills in 1960. But on the back nine his game fell apart. He drove out of bounds on one hole, then into a pond on the next. His mood was not helped by him losing a heated dispute with a rules official over where to drop his ball, and by the time he reached the 18th green, after a string of bogeys, Bolt was fuming. The tee shot required a carry over a lake and, inevitably, it did not make it to dry ground. Neither did the second ball, which was all too much for Tommy. Winding up with a swing fuelled by pure rage, Bolt hurled his driver into the water, too.

With quick thinking, a small boy in the gallery dived into the lake and amazingly retrieved the driver. He emerged from the water with the club over his head and even Bolt finally had to break into a smile as he went to thank the boy for finding his favourite club. But immediately the boy broke into a run, skipped past Bolt, sped

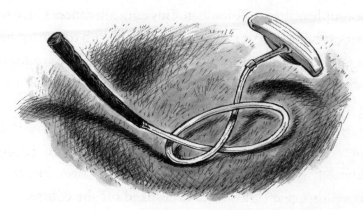

across the fairway and, after getting help over the chain-link fence enclosing the property, from another spectator, disappeared forever!

Robert Sommers:

No one could remember stronger winds than those that whipped across Hazeltine National Golf Club, near Minneapolis, during the first round of the 1970 US Open. They roared out of the northwest at thirty-five miles an hour at their weakest, and gusted over forty. They blew with such strength they almost uprooted a massive scoreboard anchored in places by six-by-six-inch pilings driven four feet into the ground.

After shooting 79 in the first round, Sam Snead tried to sneak away without signing his scorecard, which would have caused him to be disqualified, the only way he could avoid coming back again the next day. Realising what Snead was up to, Lee Trevino called, 'Sam, come back; you forgot to sign your scorecard.'

Trevino then muttered to Frank Hannigan, the USGA official checking scorecards in the scorer's tent, 'If I've gotta come back tomorrow, he's coming back, too!'

Martin Johnson: Daily Telegraph

Dateline: 2001 US Open, Southern Hills, Tulsa, Oklahoma

Tiger Woods (now ruthlessly exposed as a four-in-a-row flash in the pan) helped pull in crowds of 35,000 a day to Southern Hills, but the only chance of a crush at the gates during yesterday's 18-hole playoff between Mark Brooks and Retief Goosen would have been from people clamouring to get out.

Goosen, Brooks and Stewart Cink produced a display of putting on the 18th green on Sunday that was reminiscent of a family outing at a crazy golf course, concluding with Goosen winning this year's Jean van de Velde award for the most hapless final-hole short-circuit in a major championship. And it all ended with the most eagerly awaited golfing shoot-out in the US since someone had the bright idea of a million-dollar matchplay tournament between the world's top sixty-four players, and ended up with a final between Jeff Maggert and Andrew Magee.

The most interesting aspect of yesterday's playoff was the battle for the title of the most boring golfer to win a

major, with Brooks cast in the role of defending champion after his victory at the 1996 US PGA. With Goosen
in the opposite corner, this was sudden death at the box
office.

Goosen was once hospitalised for two months after
being struck by lightning on a course in his native South
Africa, the closest he has come to being associated with
electricity. There were anxious moments when his doctors
were searching for a pulse, as indeed golf galleries have
been doing for most of his career. Goosen is laid-back
on a golf course to the point of making Ernie Els look a
nervous wreck.

The locals were so clued up about Goosen before this
championship that he was billed all week on the media
tent scoreboard as a native of England. Even allowing
for the Americans' legendary grasp of geography – there
will be tourists wandering around London today asking
for directions to the Parthenon – this is anonymity on a
grand scale.

Goosen, whose missed two-footer for the title may
well supplant Doug Sanders' effort in the 1970 Open
as the most famous twitched putt in major championship history, registered something approaching
emotion for the first time in 72 holes, and Brooks,
looking equally bewildered as he watched it on television, had to retrieve his clubs from the boot of his
courtesy car.

All the interesting players had long since driven out of the gates, including Colin Montgomerie, who finished the tournament in a way that he may not have had in mind when he set off on Saturday with only ten competitors ahead of him. Paired for the final day with someone called Jimmy Walker, of Cibolo, Texas, it is safe to say that Monty did not enjoy a meaningless round that dragged on for four hours.

The three-balls on Thursday and Friday averaged around 5.5 hours, which makes you wonder when, if ever, professional golf will get around to docking people strokes rather than imposing occasional paltry fines, and then always involving people you have never heard of. Three Montys would nip round in a couple of hours, but if they ever put Bernhard Langer, Padraig Harrington and Miguel Jimenez in the same threesome, the caddies would not so much require a yardage chart as a sextant.

A whole generation of children is growing up in the belief that you cannot play a shot without first weighing up distance, wind direction, what you had for lunch, and where Jupiter is currently situated in relation to Venus, but then again, help might be at hand from an unexpected source. If we are about to enter a Goosen–Brooks era of world domination, no one will want to take up golf in the first place.

Robert Sommers:

The game is full of squelches, some even unintentional. Sam Snead stood banging balls on the practice tee early in the week of the US Open one year while a lone spectator stood watching him. After a time the spectator called to Sam and asked, 'When do the pros start playing?'

A little vain to begin with, Sam was naturally put off. 'I don't know,' he snarled, 'I was just sent out here to break in the course!'

Peter Dobereiner:

Bobby Cruickshank was a small, wiry Scot whose promising amateur career was interrupted by the First World War. He escaped from a German prisoner-of-war camp and soon after the war he turned professional and emigrated to the United States where he quickly won a reputation as a fine player and all-round athlete.

In the 1934 US Open Championship at Merion, Philadelphia, he was leading after two rounds and going well in the third round. His approach to the 11th hole was slightly spared and to his dismay he saw the ball falling short into the brook, which winds in front of the green.

The ball landed on a rock, which was barely covered by water, rebounded high into the air and landed on the green. Cruickshank jubilantly tossed his club into the air, tipped his cap and shouted, 'Thank you, God.'

Further expressions of gratitude were cut short as the descending club landed on top of his head and knocked him out cold!

Martin Johnson: Daily Telegraph

Dateline: 2001 US Open, Southern Hills, Tulsa, Oklahoma

More bonhomie was to follow at the 225-yard, par-three 8th, where Colin Montgomerie's dark contemplation about a tee shot falling a good twenty yards short of the putting surface was interrupted by a shout of: 'Good shot, Monty.'

The Scot pulled his tee peg from the ground and – this time getting the yardage exactly right – bounced it neatly off the top of his tormentor's head.

Barry Johnston:

Frank Urban 'Fuzzy' Zoeller Jr is one of the most popular characters in golf. He is one of only three golfers to have won the Masters at the first attempt and he also won the 1984 US Open in Mamaroneck, New York. At the 18th green on the final day, Fuzzy jokingly waved his white towel in mock surrender after Greg Norman sank a monster putt for par to tie him after 72 holes. Next day he beat Norman in the 18-hole playoff by a wide margin.

Fuzzy's easygoing rapport with the gallery has brought him a worldwide following, known as 'Fuzzy Fans'. He appreciates their loyalty and their support, and explains, 'Without the people, I'd be playing in front of trees for a couple of hundred dollars!'

He is well known for his light-hearted approach to the professional game. On one occasion he arrived at a newly designed golf course and was so unimpressed that he enquired loudly, 'Where are the windmills and animals?'

Fuzzy's attitude to golf is simple: 'I accept the fact that I'm going to miss it sometimes. I just hope I miss it where I can find it!'

Robert Sommers:

Sitting in front of his locker after the second round of the 1956 US Open, Ben Hogan fielded questions from the press. He had shot 140 for 36 holes and stood a stroke behind Peter Thomson, the young Australian who had won the previous two British Opens. As the interview progressed, a reporter asked Hogan, 'Ben, would you rather be one stroke behind right now or one stroke ahead?'

With an icy stare, meant to freeze his questioner, Hogan snarled, 'Would you rather be rich or would you rather be poor?'

Tony Jacklin:

The 1970 US Open was played at the relatively new Hazeltine Club in Chaska, Minnesota, in the great wide, wide open Midwest, 'wide open' being the operative phrase. As a fairly new course (Hazeltine had only opened in 1962) the trees and even the landscaping were not that mature, which, combined with its exposed lakeside site and the June date, made for strong winds.

It wasn't just the wind that was ruffling a few feathers. By the time we arrived for our first practice round the players, or at least some of them, were already in full gripe mode. To say Hazeltine was proving unpopular with the players is like saying the *Titanic* shipped a bit of water. Why was everybody complaining? We were all playing the same course. Dave Hill, who would eventually finish second, and who was never a man to send in diplomats when battalions of troops were available, came right out and said it was a terrible golf course, that it should be ploughed up.

'All it needs,' he added, 'is eighty acres of corn and some cows!'

For this, a funny but perhaps unwise remark, Dave earned the scorn of the local crowd. I played the third round with him, and up and down the fairways he went with the sound of the crowd mooing after him.

Dave Hill was fined $150 for his comments about the cow pasture (a fine delivered, ironically, on the birthday of Robert Trent Jones, the course's designer). Hill paid the fine practically on the spot, and then let everyone know he was tempted to pay double the amount of the fine just for the privilege of voicing his opinion about the course again!

Barry Johnston:

During the final round of the 1967 US Open at Baltusrol, in Springfield, New Jersey, Arnold Palmer and Jack Nicklaus were paired together in what soon became a duel for the championship. Palmer was ahead by one at the second hole but Nicklaus birdied the third and he was never behind again. Even though Palmer would become the first player to score less than 280 in the US Open twice, it was not enough to beat Jack Nicklaus.

However, his legion of loyal fans never gave up hope. As Nicklaus headed for a final round of 65 and a new scoring record of 275 to win his second US Open,

Arnie's Army held up signs behind the water hazards and bunkers.

They read: RIGHT HERE, JACK!

Robert Sommers:

While he had never been compared to a rocket scientist, Lou Graham, the 1975 US Open champion, had a certain earthy wisdom, at least as it related to golf. He understood it better than one might expect.

'Golf is a dumb game,' he explained. 'Hitting the ball is the fun part of it, but the fewer times you hit the ball the more fun you have. Does this make any sense?'

Barry Johnston:

After he won the 1970 US Open by an incredible seven strokes at Hazeltine National Golf Club, near Minneapolis, Tony Jacklin was presented with the famous silver trophy and a cheque for $30,000 (worth about $180,000 today). Not only had he recorded the largest winning margin for forty-nine years but he was also the first British player to win the US Open since Ted Ray in 1920. After the presentation ceremony Tony and his wife Vivien went out to celebrate with friends at dinner and the next morning they flew back to England.

Soon after they had returned home, it is said that Vivien took some of Tony's clothes round to their local dry cleaners. When they checked his suit, the cleaners were surprised to find a crumpled piece of paper had been left in one of the pockets.

It was a cheque – for $30,000!

CHARACTERS

Sam Torrance:

Brian Barnes was the biggest, most colourful character in golf at a time when there were a few more than now. He was a great player, probably better than he ever knew, a long, straight hitter with a good touch around the greens. As much as I always loved the description 'the man who sank the winning putt in the Ryder Cup', he grew to resent being introduced as 'the man who beat Jack Nicklaus twice in a day'. It remains a great feat illustrative of a temperament and talent that could have taken him to the very top, but for his well-documented drinking problem.

We both tell stories about each other at my first World Cup at Palm Springs, California, in 1976. To a Scot, the World Cup is football and just the biggest event in the world. As a Scot, playing for Scotland, I regarded golf's equivalent in a similar vein. Well, according to Barnsie, I could not get my kilt off after the gala dinner, so I walked into the cupboard, undid it and let it drop.

Barnes was intent on not spilling a drop. He had been drinking a few cold beers during the first round and I don't mean surreptitiously. Then he began to mark his ball on the green with a can of beer. Finally, he tucked a can in his shirt pocket when he was putting, swigging the liquid down to a level so that it would not pour out as he bent over.

The crowd loved it and Michelob, the sponsors, loved it. In the third round Michelob sent out a buggy with a fridge full of beer on the back!

Barry Johnston:

During the 1992 Toyota World Match Play Championship at Wentworth, Jeff Sluman came up against the defending champion, Seve Ballesteros, in the quarter-finals. It was a very windy day and the conditions were so difficult that one of Ballesteros' tee shots hit a leaderboard being held by an elderly woman. After it bounced back on to the fairway, Seve chuckled to Sluman, 'It's my grandmother!'

Sluman beat the five-time winner by two holes and went on to face Nick Faldo in the final, where he was totally overwhelmed 8 and 7 by the current Open champion. Faldo led from the first hole and at one point, in an effort to relieve his tension, Sluman enquired of a policeman, 'How's Fergie?'

Nothing the American did seemed to work. By the lunch break Faldo was already six up after 18 holes. When he was asked what he had done during the interval, Sluman replied, 'I put Vaseline on Nick's grips!'

By the 29th hole it was the end of the Burma Road for Jeff Sluman. He sighed, 'My mother told me there would be days like this!'

Barry Johnston:

Mildred 'Babe' Didrikson Zaharias was probably the greatest all-round athlete of the twentieth century. In the 1932 Los Angeles Olympics she won gold medals in the javelin and 80 metres hurdles, breaking her own world record, and a silver medal in the high jump. She also excelled at tennis, basketball, baseball, swimming, billiards and even ten-pin bowling.

After the Olympics she took up golf, hitting more than one thousand balls a day in practice. She soon won a tournament in her native Texas but it was after the war when Babe dominated the women's game, winning seventeen consecutive amateur victories, a feat that has never been equalled.

In 1947 she became the first American to win the British Ladies' Amateur Championship, at Gullane in Scotland. She was so confident in her ability that she played trick shots on some holes, to cheers from the excited spectators. When an opponent asked if she could pick up a ball from casual water, Babe replied, 'Honey, I don't mind if you have it dry-cleaned!'

After turning professional, Babe Zaharias was the top money-earner from 1948 to 1951 and won the US Women's Open three times. Before one LPGA tournament she approached some of the other players on the practice green and said, 'I don't know why you're practising so hard to finish second!'

Babe Zaharias was so strong that she was longer off the tee than most men. On one occasion, after hitting one of her trademark long drives, she was complimented on her golf swing. Babe indicated her breasts and, in her broad Texan accent, said, 'If ah didn't have these, ah'd hit it twenty yards farther!'

Robert Sommers:

Tommy Bolt was paired with Porky Oliver during the Colonial National Invitational Tournament, a big event during the 1950s. Tommy was having a terrible day, missing putts that should have fallen and threatening to snap his putter over his knee. Oliver spent a considerable part of the afternoon trying to calm him down and save the putter.

Sensing that as soon as the round ended Bolt would try for a new distance record with a thrown putter, Porky said to Bolt, 'Tommy, let me see that putter.'

Bolt handed it over . . . and *Porky* tossed it into the lake!

Barry Johnston:

Sir Winston Churchill played golf as a young man but he showed little aptitude for the game. It required too much precision. He declared, 'Playing golf is like chasing a quinine pill around a cow pasture!' Churchill preferred to play polo, because it involved riding on horseback, a much larger ball and a big mallet with which to hit it. He was also too easily distracted for golf. Before the First World War, when he was First Lord of the Admiralty in the Liberal government, Churchill used to play golf with the Prime Minister, Herbert Asquith. It is said that Asquith would deliberately get Churchill talking about his favourite subject, probably the urgent need for more battleships, and he would get so engrossed that he would forget to play another shot, much to Asquith's delight.

Churchill once observed, 'Golf is a game in which you try to put a small ball in a small hole with implements singularly unsuited to the purpose!'

Barry Johnston:

The flamboyant Texan Jimmy Demaret was one of the greatest showmen in the history of golf. He won thirty-one PGA Tour events in a career that lasted from 1935 to 1957, and, in the grey days after the Second World War, he was renowned for his loud clothes and his lively sense of humour. Before he stepped onto the 1st tee at a tournament, everyone in the gallery would be speculating, 'I wonder what he's going to wear today?'

Demaret's clothing has been described as 'the peacock-meets-plus-fours look'. His favourite colours included flaming scarlet, peach, purple, tangerine, burgundy and canary yellow, and he might easily match a rose-coloured cardigan with an electric blue shirt and green

suede shoes. In 1954 the Texan golfer was said to own 71 pairs of trousers, 55 shirts, 39 jackets, 20 sweaters, and hundreds of pairs of shoes.

Jimmy Demaret enjoyed a laugh and a drink almost as much as his golf. His maxim was, 'Get out and live. You're dead for an awful long time.'

He also claimed, 'Golf and sex are about the only things you can enjoy without being good at!'

Barry Johnston:

Brian Barnes won the Zambia Open at the Lusaka Golf Club in 1979 and again in 1981. One year during the tournament he popped into the clubhouse bar and knocked back three pints in quick succession, then looked at his watch, before heading for the door. 'I better be going now,' he said, 'I'm on the tenth tee!'

After Barnes had rolled in his putt on the last hole to win the tournament, President Kenneth Kaunda was so excited that he ran on to the green and flung his arms around Barnes, shouting, 'Well done, son!'

Barnes grinned and replied, 'Thanks, Dad!'

Sam Torrance:

Two of my best friends and tour travelling companions in what I should not really regard as the good old days

– though I do – were Irish: John O'Leary from Dublin and David Feherty from Bangor in the north.

David did not get on tour until 1980. He was not as young as some starting out but he received the same treatment from me as all the other youngsters, sharing what I knew, giving them encouragement. 'Don't be such a fairy,' I would say. 'Don't be such a Jessie.'

I certainly called Feherty a 'big Jessie' many a time. Once, memorably, when he was bitten by a snake in deepest . . . Surrey. We were playing in a money match, of course, ahead of the PGA Championship at Wentworth in 1992 – David and me against Wayne Riley and Roger Chapman. I was on my way to the 12th tee when I spotted a wee snake at the bottom of a tree. I poked it with my driver so much that it must have been well pissed off by the time Feherty arrived. He couldn't resist it. He went up there and did his David Attenborough bit. 'I'll identify this creature, no problem.'

He took a look at it, turned it over and saw it was an adder. 'That's the only poisonous snake in Britain,' he declared. He tried to flick it away but hit it fat and it wriggled up the shaft and bit him at the end of the index finger. I wasn't going to miss such an opportunity. 'You've just been bitten by the only poisonous snake in Britain!' I grinned.

'You bastard,' he snapped. 'Maybe I should go in.'

'We're two hundred pounds up,' I reminded him. 'Don't be such a Jessie.'

So he sucked the poison and spat it out and we carried on. By the next hole, he couldn't feel his finger tip. It was stiff and absolutely numb. We played another couple of holes and it got worse. His finger was now straight out and swollen like a bee sting. 'I can't feel a thing,' he moaned. 'Not even if you hit it with a hammer.'

'Put the finger on this bench,' I said and I whacked it with my driver. 'Did you feel that? No? Right, you can play.' We won the money, finished the round and headed for the St John Ambulance people.

When he finally told them he had been bitten by a snake – ninety minutes earlier – he was suddenly transported into the world of blue flashing lights, Chertsey Hospital and cortisone injections. He was admitted for the night. I bought him some grapes but ate them all before I got there.

Later I told the waiting press: 'It does not look good. Oh, you mean Feherty. I thought you meant the snake!'

Barry Johnston:

Mason Rudolph, from Clarksville, Tennessee, was one of the youngest players, at sixteen years and six days, ever to qualify to play in the US Open. He joined the PGA Tour in 1959, when he was named Rookie of the Year, and he went on to be a member of the 1971 US Ryder Cup team. He also managed the remarkable achievement of finishing in the money on the PGA Tour in fifty-two straight events.

When he was asked what professional golfers think of each other, Rudolph declared, 'Out here you've got to realise that if you take an eight on a hole, ninety per cent of the other pros don't care, and the other ten per cent wish it had been a nine!'

Barry Johnston:

Fuzzy Zoeller has been known to enjoy a drink or two after a tournament and has even discussed plans to launch his own brand of ultra-premium vodka. In the 1990s Fuzzy was talking about his early days on the US Tour when he complained that professional golf was in danger of becoming too serious:

'The younger guys don't drink. They eat their bananas and drink their fruit drinks, then go to bed. It's a *miserable* way to live!'

Barry Johnston:

David Feherty won more than $3 million in prize money as a professional golfer but he blew the lot. He is not the first sportsman, and probably not the last, to confess, 'I spent a lot of money on fast cars, women and alcohol. The rest I just squandered!'

The biggest win of Feherty's career was the 1986 Scottish Open at Haggs Castle, in Glasgow. He was awarded a huge silver cup and during the next few hours he celebrated his victory by filling it up with different types of booze and drinking it dry, several times over. Feherty woke up two days later on the 16th tee at Gleneagles, nearly fifty miles away, with no memory of how he had got there. The trophy was missing.

They never did find it!

Sandy Lyle:

Entirely self-taught, Lee Trevino opted out of the Texas education system as a fourteen-year-old to work on a driving range before enlisting in the US Marines from which he graduated on to the US Tour. Trevino went on to win six majors – two Opens, two US Opens and two US PGA titles.

The galleries loved 'Super Mex' because here was a man whose unique swing not only defied every law of nature but who also kept up a steady stream of one-liners even on his backswing. Some of these are just too good not to repeat here and, although I didn't hear Lee deliver all of them during the numerous times we played together, they certainly provide a fair reflection of the man I know, like and admire.

On his upbringing: My family was so poor they couldn't afford kids. The lady next door had me . . . By the time I was five I was working in the fields. I thought hard work was just how life was. I was twenty-one years old before I discovered Manual Labor wasn't a Mexican!

On his wealth: I'm going to win so much money this year my caddie will make it on to the top twenty money-winners' list . . . I may buy the Alamo and give it back to the Mexicans . . . You can make a lot of money in this game. Just ask my ex-wives . . . You don't know what pressure is until you've played for five bucks with only two in your pocket!

On golf-course architects: If I were designing one for myself there would be a dogleg right on every hole. And

the first hole wouldn't count – it would be a warm-up hole . . . Spyglass Hill in California? They ought to hang the man who designed it. Ray Charles could have done better!

On the Open: This is the one tournament I would play if I had to leave America a month early and swim over!

On the occasion his three playing partners all drove into the woods: What's over there . . . a nudist colony?

FORE!

P.G. Wodehouse: Ordeal by Golf

Mitchell Holmes had only one fault. He lost his temper when playing golf. He seldom played a round without becoming piqued, peeved, or – in many cases – chagrined. The caddies on our links, it was said, could always worst other small boys in verbal arguments by calling them some of the things they had heard Mitchell call his ball on discovering it in a cuppy lie. He had a great gift of language, and he used it unsparingly.

I will admit that there was some excuse for the man. He had the makings of a brilliant golfer, but a combination of bad luck and inconsistent play invariably robbed him of the fruits of his skill. He was the sort of player who does the first two holes in one under bogey and then takes an eleven at the third. The least thing upset him on the links. He missed short putts because of the uproar of the butterflies in the adjoining meadows!

Peter Alliss:

Some years ago I received a letter from Mr Roy Richardson of Kempsey, near Worcester. He was a member of the Senior Section of the Puckrup Hall Golf Club near Tewkesbury. He thought the following 'Golfer's Prayer' would amuse me:

The pro is my shepherd, I shall not slice,
He maketh me drive straight down
   the green fairways,
He leadeth me across the still water hazards,
He restoreth my approach shots,
He leadeth me down the paths of
   accuracy for my game's sake.
Yea, though I chip through the rough in
   the shadow of the sand traps,
I fear no bogeys, for his advice is with me.
He prepareth a strategy for me in the
   presence of my opponents,
He anointeth my head with confidence.
The cup will not run over,
Surely birdies and eagles shall follow
   me all the rounds of my life
And I will score in the low 80s for ever.

Bruce Forsyth:

My wife Wilnelia has accounted for two embarrassing moments – both, I hasten to add, before she knew as much about the game as she does now. The first was in Florida, when I asked her to ride in a buggy with me so that she could see what golf was all about. I wasn't playing well that day and was just primed to hit what I hoped would be a first-class rescue shot. At that precise moment, Wilnelia called out, 'Come on, Brucie baby!'

I just wish I had a keepsake picture of the look I gave her as the ball disappeared into the trees!

The second occasion was in Spain. I was playing in a competition and I couldn't find the ball in the rough. Quite a few people were trying to help, including Wilnelia. All of a sudden I heard her shout, 'I've found it, Bruce. I've found it!' I was thrilled – until I turned round. There she was triumphantly holding the ball, waving it above her head.

That moment earned me a two-shot penalty!

Barry Johnston:

CBS Sports golf analyst David Feherty is well known for his outspoken comments and his sharp wit. After he retired as a professional golfer in 1997, he observed, 'The world's number one tennis player spends ninety per cent of his time winning, while the world's number one golfer spends ninety per cent of his time losing. Golfers are great losers!'

Tom O'Connor:

From my home I am only a short distance from many great clubs – Sunningdale, Wentworth and so on. There is plenty of scope for golfing enjoyment and for meeting interesting people.

Take Paul, a long-time member of Wentworth, a good player and a gentleman, always polite and a marvellous teller of tales.

I'll never forget a 'friendly' we played when, after 13 holes, he'd kindly allowed me to be all square, such was his prowess. We were standing on the 14th tee of the west course facing 160 yards, all uphill – not an easy prospect.

Paul pointed out the greenkeeper's hut on the right of the fairway and asked if I had heard the sad story about it. I fell for it and said, 'No, please tell me . . .'

Apparently, Paul went on, nine years before, in a Sunday morning mixed foursome, a man had teed off, duffed his shot and his ball had landed behind the shed.

'Play it out sideways to the fairway,' he told his wife, 'and I'll try to chip us somewhere near the flag.'

But she had other ideas. 'There's a door at this end,' she said. 'If there's one at the other end, open it and I'll try to play through.'

For some reason he complied, opened the far door and watched her strike an iron straight at the door frame. The ricochet hit her between the eyes and killed her outright. Her husband understandably never played again.

Eight years later, however, he was persuaded to go out on another Sunday morning round, 'just to give it a try'. And by a billion to one chance his ball performed exactly the same feat on the 14th and landed behind the self-same shed again.

'Shall I try to play it through if you hold the door open?' enquired his new lady partner.

'Get lost!' he replied. 'Last time I took a seven . . . !'

Sandy Lyle:

I have made myself laugh on occasion, such as the time I had to turn down a dinner invitation to No. 10 Downing Street where Margaret Thatcher was entertaining George Bush and I was famously quoted as saying: 'I was really sorry because I know they are also very busy people.'

I knew what I meant, just as I did when I won the Suntory World Match Play – on my fifth attempt – and told a startled audience, which included our Japanese sponsors, that 'I like playing in Japan because I enjoy Chinese food so much!'

Tim Brooke-Taylor:
THE GOLFER'S HALL OF FAME

This is my hall of fame and I make no apologies for including a name that may be unfamiliar. Lieutenant-Colonel Spooner was a daredevil American 'stunt' golfer who flew for many years with a barnstorming circus and adopted much of the same devil-may-care philosophy

towards his golf game. He would often encourage new or unsuspecting playing partners to lie on the grass, a ball balanced precariously on the end of their nose, where-upon he would take out a stout two-wood and attempt to drive the ball clear from its impromptu tee.

'He's done it again!' became a common cry from the clubhouses around Spooner's native Wisconsin as another hapless victim staggered into the clubroom nurs-ing a bleeding nose and badly bruised lip.

Perhaps the Colonel's most famous stunt came during a 1928 'novelty' contest in which players were encour-aged to compete for the most original round of golf. As the quaint and colourfully dressed competitors gathered on the 1st tee ready to perform their exotic tricks, a loud roar suddenly erupted behind them, and looking round in horror they were just able to dive for cover as Spooner burst over the horizon in a frail boxplane, one hand on the rudder while the other thrashed around frantically beneath the aircraft with a seven-iron, gamely trying to tee off a nearby ball. The fact that Spooner insisted on playing out the entire round in this airborne manner says a great deal about the man's raw courage.

Certainly the vision of him swooping down low over a three-foot putt with engine screeching and putter dangling feebly from outstretched hand will live forever in the memory of those lucky enough to see it!

Barry Johnston:

A golfer was hitting a few shots on the practice green when he saw a shifty looking young man approaching him. 'Hey!' said the man. 'Do you want to see something amazing?'

The golfer, annoyed at being interrupted, snapped, 'What is it?'

'It's a special golf ball,' said the man, confidently. 'You can never lose it!'

The golfer snorted in disbelief. 'What do you mean, you can never lose it? What if you hit it into the water?'

'That's no problem,' said the man. 'It floats, then it detects where the shore is and spins towards it.'

'Well, what if you hit it into the woods?'

'Easy,' said the man. 'It emits a beeping sound and you can find it with your eyes closed.'

'Okay,' said the golfer, now impressed. 'But what if your round goes late and it starts getting dark?'

'No problem, sir,' said the man. 'The ball glows in the dark. I'm telling you, you can never lose this golf ball!'

That clinched it. The golfer bought the ball on the spot. As the man pocketed the money, the golfer asked him, 'Just one question. Where did you get it?'

'I found it!'

Michael Green: The Art of Coarse Golf

Postal Golf was invented by my friend Askew and myself for use during the depths of winter, but some people might prefer it to the ordinary game even when the weather is good.

The rules are simple. A course is selected and each player has a card. The player who has the honour goes into his garden and drives a plastic practice ball, and on the basis of the stroke makes an estimation of what would have happened to the ball.

He then sends a postcard to his opponent, saying for instance: HAVE JUST DRIVEN TWO HUNDRED YARDS BUT SLICED INTO ROUGH GRASS ON FIRST.

His opponent replies, and then both go on to their irons. Putting is done in the dining-room, using a tumbler on the carpet.

This harmless and amusing game was, however, wrecked by the sheer egotism of Askew. While I honestly recorded each slice, hook or dunch (the penalty for slicing or hooking was the compulsory use of an eight-iron for the next shot, with subsequent loss of distance), Askew's overweening sense of his own importance led him to make fantastic claims.

It all began with a postcard reading: HAVE JUST HIT THREE HUNDRED YARD DRIVE STRAIGHT DOWN MIDDLE.

When I replied: HAVE LANDED TWO FEET FROM PIN WITH THREE-IRON, Askew started claiming a succession of birdies, first lulling me into a false sense of security by admitting that he was in a bunker and then claiming to have sunk the bunker shot.

We finally abandoned the game when, after I had clearly won a hole, he sent a postcard: YOU ARE PENALISED TWO STROKES BECAUSE YOUR BALL STRUCK MINE ON THE GREEN.

We did not talk to each other for some time after that but I still think the game could be successful, provided it is not played between two psychopaths!

Jeremy Hanley:

From 1990 to 1993, I was honoured to be the Under-Secretary of State for Northern Ireland. We worked all the hours that God sent, but the need to relax, exercise and enjoy oneself was still important, even at a particularly tricky time in the province's history. Happily, a government minister could always find a four for golf – his two security guards and his private secretary (the 'Bernard' to his 'Hacker').

One sunny evening, we reckoned we could grab a quick nine holes at Clandeboye, near Bangor. I drove off and, as usual, hooked the ball into the deep rough down in a woody hollow, about 150 yards from the tee. To save time, I set off to try to find the ball, with Stevie, my lead escort, executing a perfect drive towards the green. As I got down towards the trees, I heard what was quite clearly the click of an Armalite cocking, from behind the clump.

Trained in such matters, I immediately threw myself flat on the ground and shouted the code word, 'Stevie!' and he charged towards me, throwing his clubs in the air, grabbing his Heckler from his bag as he ran. A second later, my ball came from behind the nearest tree and made a gentle arc onto the fairway. From behind the thicket, a squaddie in full camouflage appeared, and said, 'We can't have ministers charging around the undergrowth in Northern Ireland, sir.'

He then blew a whistle and down the length of the fairway five more soldiers emerged from the rough, clearly moving from hole to hole ahead of us.

I seemed to end up on the fairway pretty regularly after that, and suffice to say, that was the first and only time I broke 50 for the outward nine!

Barry Johnston:

One night, during dinner in a Southport hotel, a female admirer selected a carnation from the table display in front of her and asked a waiter to take it over to Major John Bywaters, the secretary of the Professional Golfers Association, who was dining at a nearby table.

According to Peter Dobereiner, Bywaters acknowledged the gift with an extravagant bow, then dunked the carnation into his claret and ate it!

Tony Jacklin:

In 1988 I decided to accept an invitation to play in a tournament called the Four Stars up at Moor Park. At one of the dinners they had for the event, I was at the head table. Terry Wogan was there. Joan Collins was down the table, and she was sitting close to Bill Wiggins, a bit of a man about town and something of a partier. Princess Margaret was near me, as was good old Jimmy Tarbuck, a pal of mine forever who is one of the funniest men in Britain. At one point, Princess Margaret, who was a good sort, noticed Joan Collins and Bill Wiggins getting on rather well. She leaned over to Jimmy.

'Mr Tarbuck,' she said. 'Who's the gentleman with Mrs Collins?'

Jimmy said, 'It's Bill Wiggins, Ma'am.'

Princess Margaret nodded. 'I see. And what does he do?'

Jimmy, who knew Margaret well enough to say this, leaned in close. 'Well . . . I think he gives her one, Ma'am.'

'Really.' Princess Margaret sat back, let the lightest smile cross her lips. 'He must be very good at it!'

John Betjeman:

SEASIDE GOLF

How straight it flew, how long it flew,
It clear'd the rutty track
And soaring, disappeared from view
Beyond the bunker's back —
A glorious, sailing, bounding drive
That made me glad I was alive.

Fore!

And down the fairway, far along
It glowed a lonely white;
I played an iron sure and strong
And clipp'd it out of sight,
And spite of grassy banks between
I knew I'd find it on the green.

And so I did. It lay content
Two paces from the pin;
A steady putt and then it went
Oh, most surely in.
The very turf rejoiced to see
That quite unprecedented three.

Ah! Seaweed smells from sandy caves
And thyme and mist in whiffs,
Incoming tide, Atlantic waves
Slapping the sunny cliffs,
Lark song and sea sounds in the air
And splendour, splendour everywhere.

EUROPEAN TALES

Michael Parkinson:

It was in Spain that my reluctant conversion to golf began. My teacher was Mr James Tarbuck, a passionate advocate of the game and a very fine player. He arranged my inaugural round. At the third hole he suggested I drive first and showed me the line. The shot looked difficult and dangerous because it involved driving over the top of a group of workmen.

'Shout fore,' said Jimmy. I did and was perturbed to see the men return my warning with what I took to be offensive gestures.

'Tell them to sod off,' said my friend. So I did and they retreated, shaking their fists.

I settled down and hit the shot in the direction specified by my partner. I looked to him for praise.

'Good shot,' he said, 'except that the hole is down there!' pointing in the opposite direction.

The most humiliating part was having to retrieve my ball watched by the workmen I had so abused and who were not used to seeing their course played that way!

Alex Hay:

Joining Dunham Forest Golf Club introduced me to many lasting friends and great characters – none more so than one real eccentric by the name of David Norton, whose family had prospered in the great steel-mill days of Salford in Lancashire. David introduced me to golfing abroad.

The Nortons had a lovely home in Le Touquet and David would move over there every August to join Monique, his fairly excitable French wife, and their children, who spent the summer in France.

On those glorious August days, when I became an annual house guest, it was a joy to play on La Mer, one of Europe's best links courses. We were always joined on the 9th green by Monsieur Charles, a charming man who ran Le Manoir, a superb building used as a clubhouse and restaurant, and who would drive his car along a well-worn track out across the dunes with two bottles of champagne and a tray of smoked salmon sandwiches in a hamper tucked in the boot. This would sustain us until were safely back at Le Manoir for lunch.

Monique suggested it would be a good idea to have a birthday tea for Christopher, her eldest son, who would be twelve, and ask Le Manoir's chef to bake a special birthday cake big enough to feed an army of nephews and nieces (her whole family used to descend on Le Touquet for the summer). David, she suggested, should order this, after we had completed our round of golf for the following day; this he did, but omitted to point out to Charles that the large birthday cake was for his son and not for himself.

I shall never forget Charles' expression when the cars spilled out the hordes of children on to the steps of Le Manoir, which was matched moments later when the chef appeared around the kitchen door and found out this was a children's party and not one for David's normal colleagues. David was immediately taken to one side, where it was explained to him that the cake was definitely an adult's cake and was certainly not a children's cake. Assurances were given by David, who was eyeing up the work of art on its silver platter, that this was no problem; neither the chef nor Charles would be held responsible. What's more, David claimed, 'So long as no one tells Monique the difference will never be noticed.'

The chef rolled his eyes.

The first suggestion that this statement was not totally accurate came when Monique asked the head waiter if someone had spilled some brandy at lunchtime in the room, which she claimed, reeked of it. The second came when a six-year-old cousin, midway through her first portion of cake, toppled from her chair to the floor, out for the count.

'Poor thing,' said David, 'she's tired out.' Turning to the child's mother: 'You French keep children up too late at night!'

That certainly proved to be correct that evening, for almost the entire group spent most of it being sick.

Our cake was completely devoured, mainly by the

fathers, who had reluctantly given up a sporting afternoon to attend with their offspring and were now enthusiastically tucking in!

Tom Cox: Bring Me the Head of Sergio Garcia!

When I was a player on the 2007 Europro Tour, some in-vogue examples of clichéd exclamatory banter (and their translations) included:

Taxi! My putt has gone past the hole by quite some distance. It's like when a vehicle you are trying to hail doesn't bother stopping for you, but with a ball and grass instead of a car and a road.

Grow . . . Some . . . Effing . . . Bollocks! My putt has come up some way short of the hole, and as a result I am now quite understandably questioning my masculinity.

It's on the dance floor! My ball is not particularly close to the hole, but it has arrived on the green safely.

H2O! I have put the ball into the water. I am sad.

Luckier than a queer with two arseholes! I did not hit a very good shot there, but, unexpectedly, it has worked out well.

About as much use as a chocolate fireman! I did not hit a very good shot there, and it has not worked out well.

I tried to keep in the spirit of things, wheeling out a few old aphorisms, but it quickly became apparent that *Over the cellophane bridge!* was just, like, so 1992. Sometimes, to keep myself amused, I would invent entirely new, and utterly meaningless, golfing phrases – e.g. *Straight off the lunchbox!* or *Damn, that's the third Tarbuck I've hit today!* – but these did not seem to catch on either!

Michael Parkinson:

In Marbella we once organised a competition for the Worst Golfing Experience of the Week, to find the person who played the round that made him wish he had never taken up golf. It was won by a gentleman from Glamorgan who went round in 120 – including a spectacular 15 on a par-three where he had some trouble with a bunker – and threw his golf bag into a nearby lake, not realising he had put his car keys and his traveller's cheques in one of the pockets. He slipped a disc while trying to retrieve it and when he got back to the hotel discovered his girlfriend (made wanton by his absence and too much sangria) in a romantic dalliance with a Spanish crimper.

Needless to say he did not turn up to receive his prize, being under heavy sedation in a darkened room, safe from the game that had proved to be his undoing!

Martin Johnson: Sunday Times

Dateline: 2009 European Open, London Club, Kent

Christian Cévaër of France and Jeev Milkha Singh of India are three shots clear of the field going into today's final round of the European Open, but the leader will want considerably more daylight than that when he clambers onto the 18th tee this afternoon. A good caddie never leaves anything to chance when it comes to packing the golf bag, and after pulling the head cover off the driver, he might also be handing the boss some rosary beads and a bottle of smelling salts.

Jack Nicklaus must have been in one of his less sunny moods when he designed the final hole at the London Club in Kent. It's 417 yards worth of malice, with water on the left, and the kind of rough on the right that suggests enough angry hacking with the niblick might lead to the discovery of a long-lost pygmy tribe. Throw in a biffing breeze, and it all added up to 69 of Europe's best golfers playing the 18th in a combined aggregate of, wait for it, 78-over-par.

Sergio Garcia's triple bogey seven wasn't quite the worst score on the hole yesterday, but it put an end to hopes of European Open glory for him on a day when 23,650 spectators flooded the course and gave the place the feel of a major championship. And when it feels like a major, Garcia usually feels some pain.

It's now more than a decade since Garcia threatened to ignite a rivalry with Tiger Woods not seen since Nicklaus and Tom Watson in the 1970s, but the Spaniard, in relative terms, has become a matador trying to despatch the bull with a cocktail stick. In fact, the only area in which Sergio has not come up short is in the excuse department, which is firmly in the 'por favor senor, el perro se comio mis deberes' ('please sir, the dog ate my homework') class.

The best on a long list came after he needed a par at the 18th to win the 2007 Open at Carnoustie but took five before losing the playoff to Padraig Harrington. It was, he explained, all the fault of a caddie in the group ahead taking so long to rake a bunker that it affected his rhythm, just as it did again a couple of months ago when his girlfriend, Greg Norman's daughter, pulled the plug on their relationship.

There wasn't, it appears, any particular reason, although maybe it was because the poor girl likes a conversation, and was unable to get a word in edgeways.

Garcia is a compulsive talker out on the course, even to his golf ball, which he commands – always in English – to 'get left', 'get right', 'get up' and 'get down'.

Golf ball technology has come a long way, but we're still a long way from one which sprouts ears, and yesterday, Sergio's wasn't listening!

Bruce Forsyth:

I can be a bit of a 'Victor Meldrew' on the course. But that's not surprising, because I am the unluckiest golfer in the world. '*Look* at that . . . *Look* what's happened to my ball . . .' I carry on ad nauseam. On one occasion I was playing with Jimmy Tarbuck in Sotogrande, Spain, and before we started to play, Jimmy straight up-front, said, 'Okay, Bruce, we haven't played for a while, so *no* moaning. You moan so much, it drives us all mad.'

'Okay,' I said, suitably contrite. 'I *won't* moan. No matter what happens, I *will not* moan.'

We reached the third hole, not a very long hole, all hit pretty good drives, and it was my turn to play. There were bunkers all around the green and one right in front of the flag. Behind this bunker, a rake had been stuck in the ground in an upright position. This was not 'par for the course' because people usually lay rakes down.

'Now look,' I said to Jimmy, 'I haven't moaned up till now, have I? Even though I shouldn't have gone in that bunker in the last hole, I didn't moan, did I?'

'No,' he said warily. 'You didn't moan, Bruce.'

'Well,' I said, 'I'm *not* going to moan now. But look . . . *if* I hit that rake and, let's face it, the handle of the rake is only about an inch wide, I'm going to have a moan.'

'Okay,' he said resigned, '*if* you hit the rake . . . But never mind the bloody rake, just hit the ball.'

I hit the ball with an eight-iron and up it went into the air. It was coming down beautifully, heading straight for the green, when, lo and behold, it hit the rake and bounced back into the bunker.

Jimmy looked at me, I looked at him, and neither of us could believe it. Defeated, Jimmy said: 'Okay, Bruce, you can have a bloody good moan now.'

Did I? What do you think!

Barry Johnston:

Belgian professional Nic Vanhootegem played so slowly at the 2001 European Tour qualifying school that Martin Johnson protested:

'Caterpillars were turning into butterflies in the time it took him to play some of his shots and he even tossed up bits of grass to check the wind before he disappeared into the trees for a call of nature!'

Ronnie Corbett:

My dad was a great fan of Henry Cotton. He admired everything about him – his swing, his look and his tremendous style. The only golf lesson he ever had in his life was from Henry and that was when I was very young, shortly after Henry won his first Open in 1934. Right to the end of his days, Henry was always keen to earn a few extra quid, even though his wife Toots was extremely wealthy, so he used to do these coaching sessions for members of the public.

Because of my dad and this famous lesson, it was especially lovely for me that I eventually became a friend of Henry Cotton. It was in 1969, on my first holiday in the Algarve, in Portugal, with my wife Anne and our two girls.

Henry Cotton was the pro at the nearby golf course at Penina, which he had designed himself – in fact he was a pioneer in making Portugal a great golfers' resort. While we were in our villa, Jimmy Tarbuck was on holiday in an hotel in the area and together we decided to ring up Henry and ask if we could play his course. He was very welcoming and invited us for drinks and then to dinner at an hotel.

So we went for drinks at Henry's house, which was as elegant as he was. It was beautifully furnished and there was a particular reason for this. In his younger days, when he was at the height of his golfing powers, Henry used to play very serious gambling golf matches with some of the most swish Bond Street dealers. Instead of playing for money, he would play for a pair of Louis XIV chairs, or a Georgian side table or an oil painting. He once confessed to me that he found he was practising harder for the furniture than he was for the serious competitions. I suppose it concentrates the mind when there's a Hepplewhite cabinet hanging on the last four-teen-foot putt.

The next day Jimmy and I arrived at the course for our game of golf. Henry met us there and told us, 'As a special favour, I am going to give you the services of my caddie, Pacifico.' The unusual thing about this particular caddie was that he was a donkey. Henry had rescued him from some cruel farmer and now looked after him and spoiled him like a favourite poodle, feeding him on Polo mints and all sort of other treats. Pacifico always carried his clubs and knew that he wasn't allowed to walk on the greens or the tees. This time he was carrying our golf bags, like panniers, Jimmy's on one side and mine on the other.

'All right, I'll leave you in the hands of Pacifico,' Henry said, going off back home. Probably going to admire his golfing trophies – including most of his furniture. Jimmy and I were tremendously pleased with ourselves as we made our way to the 1st tee, with the donkey following behind.

'Would you ever believe it?' we said. 'Here we are playing the great Henry Cotton's very own course, having dined with him last night, after having drinks in his very own house, and now he has given us his very own donkey, this wonderful Pacifico, to carry our clubs. Who'd have thought that two working-class boys like us . . .'

We would have continued with our eulogy, but we were interrupted by a powerful gushing noise. We turned round and saw Pacifico peeing copiously on the edge of the 1st tee. That seemed to be his opening comment on our presence. It went on for a very long time while we stood and waited in awe and humility.

When he had finished, we found a dry area of the tee and prepared to play our first shots. Pacifico gazed into the distance, adopting a detached attitude, as Jimmy and I twitched and fidgeted and shifted our weight from one foot to another in preparation. My shot skimmed off to the right and Jimmy's went in the opposite direction. Pacifico ambled off and stood by the first ball, and then he made his way to the second ball. There was something about that amble – a touch of hauteur. Like a waiter in a smart restaurant returning to the kitchen, letting you know that your choice of wine has failed to impress him.

We went to play our second shots, determined that this time we would impress our caddie. We did a lot of that business of shading our eyes and looking towards the horizon as if we were about to discover new lands – or at least send the ball a pretty considerable distance. I was doing some graceful, Henry Cotton-ish practice swings when Jimmy suddenly said, 'Where's Pacifico?'

I stopped in mid-swing and looked about. Our caddie was no longer with us.

'There he is,' said Jimmy, pointing.

And there he was, trotting off into the woods in the distance with our golf bags wobbling about on his back.

We ran after him, shouting things like, 'Come back, you silly ass!' but it was no good. Pacifico made it quite clear that he did not want to keep company with us.

We had to make do without a caddie after that!

THE MASTERS

Barry Johnston:

One year during the Masters there was a severe weather warning. Lightning flashes lit up the sky above Augusta as tournament officials hurriedly sent vans on to the course to evacuate the players. Gary Player was standing on the 11th tee when he was rescued and later he revealed that his first thought as he climbed into the van was, 'My, that's considerate of them.'

His second thought was, 'Yeah, but what about the forty thousand spectators!'

Robert Sommers:

During his long and colourful career, Tom Weiskopf placed second in four Masters, but he never won. Gradually he cut back on his tournament golf and began doing television commentary. He was in the television booth when Jack Nicklaus won the 1986 tournament in one of the game's major surprises. As Nicklaus lined up his putt on the 16th green, an announcer asked Weiskopf what Jack was thinking of at that moment.

Without a pause, Weiskopf said over the air, 'If I knew what was going through Jack Nicklaus's head, I would have *won* this golf tournament!'

Barry Johnston:

Jimmy Demaret was the first player to win the Masters three times – in 1940, 1947 and 1950. Gene Sarazen won the Masters once in 1935 and Byron Nelson won it twice in 1937 and 1942, and they both have bridges named after them at the Augusta National Golf Club.

Demaret complained, 'I won three times and I never even got an outhouse!'

Robert Sommers:

Looking ahead to the day when he could retire, George Archer, who won the 1969 Masters, complained, 'Baseball players quit playing and take up golf. Basketball players quit and take up golf. Football players quit and take up golf. What are we supposed to take up when *we* quit?'

Barry Johnston:

The 1967 Masters was the first golf tournament to be televised live from the United States to Europe. It was won by Gay Brewer Jr, who had finished third the previous year after an 18-hole playoff with Tommy Jacobs and the eventual winner, Jack Nicklaus.

Brewer, from Lexington, Kentucky, was a popular figure on the PGA Tour, known for his unorthodox swing and his fund of jokes and stories, but the other players needed to keep an eye on their clubs. According to Jack Nicklaus, 'Gay would walk up to you, look inside your bag, and say, "Hey, that's a great looking club. Can I try it?" If he did, there was a good chance he would never return it. Gay must have had the largest collection of borrowed clubs anyone's ever seen!'

Gay Brewer had such an unusual swing that Dave Hill once remarked, 'He swings the club in a figure eight. If you didn't know better, you'd swear he was trying to kill snakes!'

Peter Alliss:

After Sam Snead had won the Rancho Santa Fe Open in 1937 a friend brought him a cutting from a newspaper of him holding the trophy on high. The paper? The *New York Times*. When Sam saw it he remarked, 'Hey, how'd they get the picture of me? I ain't never been to New York.' Such was the then simplicity of Sam Snead, but his lack of education didn't stop him becoming an enormously wealthy man, owning huge tracts of land in Florida, and it was said that much of the land he did own was where the Disney organisation have their vast playground today. If so, goodness knows how much money Sam left, and I often wonder to whom?

I met Sam Snead at the Masters just after his seventieth birthday. I asked him how he was and what it was like to be seventy.

He replied, 'Never trust a fart, always take a pee when you can and if you get an erection, use it even if you're alone.'

Not quite Homer or Shakespeare but he was making a point, in fact three!

Barry Johnston:

In the final round of the 1989 Masters, Scott Hoch held a one-stroke lead over Nick Faldo as they walked to the 17th tee. He remembers a fan yelling out, 'You need just two pars to win the Masters!' and from then on his game fell apart. His tee shot hit a tree and rebounded on to the 15th fairway, then he missed a four-foot par putt to end up tied with Faldo. It went to a sudden-death playoff but all was not lost. At the first hole, on the 10th green, Hoch had a two-foot putt that would have clinched him the win. He circled the ball and examined all the angles. He thought to himself, 'Man, I'm going to win the Masters.'

Ben Crenshaw was watching the playoff on television in the clubhouse and cried out in frustration, 'Jeez, just hit it! I don't want to see any more golf shots today.' Hoch's putt rolled right past the hole. Crenshaw declared, 'Like my dad says, "Good Godal-mighty!"'

At the next hole Nick Faldo sank a thirty-foot birdie putt to win the first of his three green jackets.

Afterwards Hoch joked, although he might have been serious, 'I'm glad I don't carry a gun with me!'

Barry Johnston:

Before the start of the 1986 Masters, the veteran golf writer Tom McCollister penned an article in the *Atlanta Journal-Constitution* describing Jack Nicklaus as 'gone, done'. Nicklaus was then forty-six years old and had not won a major for five years. Indeed he had won only two tournaments in half a decade. One of Jack's best friends, John Montgomery, who was staying with him in

Augusta, cut out the article and taped it to the fridge in their kitchen. Every morning Nicklaus saw it at breakfast and it made him ever more determined to prove McCollister wrong.

Nicklaus recalls, 'I kept thinking all week, "Through, washed up, huh?" I sizzled for a while. But then I said to myself, "I'm not going to quit now, playing the way I'm playing. I've played too well, too long, to let a shorter period of bad golf be my last."'

In the final round on Sunday, Nicklaus shot a remarkable 7-under-par 65 to win his sixth green jacket and become the oldest player ever to win the Masters. At the press conference afterwards, Nicklaus called out, 'Where's Tom McCollister?' When he saw the journalist, Jack smiled and said, 'Thank you, Tom!'

'Glad I could help!' replied McCollister, as the whole room burst into laughter.

Later Nicklaus reflected on winning his eighteenth major at the age of forty-six and said, 'I finally found that guy I used to know on the golf course. It was me!'

Robert Sommers:

With one round to play in the 1976 Masters, Raymond Floyd led Jack Nicklaus by eight strokes and Larry Ziegler by nine. Approaching Ziegler, a reporter asked, 'What would you have to shoot tomorrow to win?'

Ziegler thought for a moment and answered, 'Raymond Floyd.'

Barry Johnston:

The Argentinian Roberto De Vicenzo won more than 230 tournaments worldwide during his long career, including the 1967 Open Championship, but he will always be remembered for his misfortune in the 1968 Masters. De Vicenzo played one of the best final rounds in major championship history, shooting 31 on the front nine at Augusta and finishing with a 65. It was his forty-fifth birthday. He thought he was heading for a playoff for the championship with Bob Goalby but he made an elementary error. He did not check his scorecard before signing it. On the par-four 17th hole, De Vicenzo had made a birdie, but his playing partner Tommy Aaron accidentally entered a '4' instead of a '3' and De Vicenzo signed the incorrect scorecard.

Under the Rules of Golf, the higher score had to stand, and De Vicenzo officially lost by one stroke. His fellow pro Jimmy Demaret commented, 'Twenty-five million people saw Roberto birdie the seventeenth hole. I think it would hold up in court.' But it was Bob Goalby who was handed the legendary green jacket.

Afterwards De Vicenzo famously exclaimed to reporters, 'What a stupid I am!'

He went on to win many other tournaments but when

he finally retired, the Argentinian said, 'Next time I come back as a golf writer. No three putts. Never miss a cut. And somebody else pays!'

Barry Johnston:

When Fuzzy Zoeller strolled up the 18th fairway at Augusta for his final appearance at the Masters in 2009, he received a standing ovation from the cheering spectators. The gallery favourite from southern Indiana was reduced to tears and later described it as 'the greatest thrill I've ever had in my life'.

After shooting 79-76, Fuzzy completed his thirtieth Masters by thanking his loyal fans. He said, 'Life is not a bowl full of cherries. There is good and bad stuff. I just hope everybody has had fun because I've enjoyed my ride.' Reflecting on his victory in the 1979 Masters, Zoeller said, 'I've never been to heaven, and thinking back on my life, I probably won't get a chance to go. I guess the Masters is as close as I'm going to get!'

He added, 'I like to see people smile. I'm miserable enough having to chase my ugly golf shots!'

Sandy Lyle:

Just as the Masters is by invitation only, so membership of Augusta National is granted to a select few only. It may be the closest thing to heaven in many ways for a golfer, but it is just about as hard to become a member. For many years Clifford Roberts ruled the club like a sporting dictator, deciding who should be admitted and, more importantly, who should be excluded. If Roberts decided you had overstayed your welcome in the members' lounge, out you went with no notification and certainly no appeal.

According to clubhouse legend, one member rang up Augusta to book a round and to reserve one of the luxury cabins, only for the switchboard operator to put him straight through to Clifford Roberts.

'Is there a problem?'

'Only that you are no longer a member.'

'For what reason, Cliff?'

'Non-payment of your bill.'

'But I haven't received a bill.'

'Exactly, only members receive bills!'

Even President Eisenhower found his role as the most powerful man in the world ended at the clubhouse door. Ike was forever driving into a tree at the edge of the 17th fairway and pleaded with Roberts on many an occasion to have the offending pine chopped down, or at the very least uprooted and moved to another location.

Roberts's reply came in the form of a discreet plaque embedded in the bark: Ike's Tree.

Barry Johnston:

Many American golfers consider Augusta National to be the most hallowed golf course in the United States, if not the world, but apparently not Boo Weekley. In 2008 the thirty-four year old from Florida made his first appearance at the Masters and when he was asked by the assembled press corps how he felt after his first practice round at Augusta, Weekley replied, 'I wasn't in awe, by no means. It's just another bunch of trees and a golf course.' Seeing their stunned reaction, he added quickly, 'But it's a nice golf course!'

He confessed that he had no idea which holes constituted Amen Corner and even wished that he was back at home, saying, 'I'd rather be catching a ten-pounder!'

When a golf correspondent enquired if he had developed any special tactics for playing in his first Masters, Weekley simply shrugged and said, 'It's caveman golf. Hit it, find it, hit it again!'

Nick Faldo:

On the Saturday evening of the 1989 Masters at Augusta, I took two English friends who had come over to support me out to dinner at Michael's Restaurant. There we fell into conversation with two women – typical Georgia gals complete with Southern drawl – at the next table, who had been intrigued by our English accents. Baby Doll (and I kid you not) told us that her companion, the fragrant Mary-Lou, was off to New York the following weekend on a shopping expedition.

'An ah'm tellin' you, Mary-Lou, you gotta be *reee-ahl* careful in that Big Apple.'

'Why's that, Baby Doll?'

''Cos in New York, Mary-Lou, they've got guys who go down on guys.'

'Hmmm, whaddya call those type of guys, Baby Doll?'

'They're call homo*say*xuals, Mary-Lou. An' you gotta be even more careful, 'cos in New York, they've got gals who go down on gals.'

'And what are they called, Baby Doll?'

'They're called *lez*bayans, Mary-Lou.'

'Baby Doll, in New York, don't they have guys who go down on gals?'

'Yes they do, Mary-Lou.'

'So what are they called, Baby Doll?'

'Hmmmm. Precious, Mary-Lou, precious!'

Barry Johnston:

In 2009 Gary Player competed in his fifty-second and final Masters at the age of seventy-three. This remarkable feat meant that he had spent a total of fifty-two weeks – one whole year of his life – playing at Augusta National.

He donned the coveted green jacket three times, in 1961, 1974 and 1978.

His local caddie at the 1978 Masters was Eddie McCoy. When Player arrived at Augusta he found that McCoy was visibly upset. He told his boss, 'You got to win this tournament, man. I'm in trouble, and I need a new house.' Player never did learn what kind of trouble his caddie was in, but it must have been serious. When the South African came from seven shots behind to win on the Sunday, Eddie McCoy was ecstatic.

Player recalls, 'There's a picture taken just after I holed a fifteen-footer on eighteen. In it, you see Eddie flying toward me like Batman, with an expression on his face as though he'd just won the lottery!'

Sandy Lyle:

Chi Chi Rodriguez said, 'One year I was so nervous about playing the Masters I drank a bottle of rum before I played. I shot the happiest eighty-three of my life!'

Barry Johnston:

Arnold Palmer and Tiger Woods were playing a practice round at Augusta, when Tiger's tee shot at the 16th missed the fairway and landed in the rough. A tall pine tree stood directly between his ball and the green.

Tiger spent a couple of minutes looking at his shot, then turned to Arnie and asked, 'How would you play this one? Lay up and take the extra stroke?'

Palmer paused thoughtfully and then replied, 'You know, when I was your age, I would hit the ball right over that tree.'

Tiger, not wanting to be shown up by old Arnie, proceeded to hit the ball hard and high, but not high enough. The ball smacked into the top of the tree trunk, bounced off, and thudded back to the ground not far from where it started.

Arnold Palmer smiled broadly and added, 'Of course, when I was your age, that tree was only three feet tall!'

ON THE BOX

Peter Alliss:

After Dave Marr's sudden departure from ABC television in the States, he joined us as a golf commentator at the BBC. This was a good break for the BBC. Although we could not match the ABC fees, it was an opportunity for him to enjoy club-class air fares, decent hotels and several thousands of pounds for each visit to our shores, which eventually became about half a dozen each year. It took him some time to get into our system. He wasn't used to the expansiveness of having time to elaborate on various aspects of the game, but he gradually understood that he would have time to finish a sentence and trot out his homespun philosophy, which I loved.

Dave Marr had been a top-class American tournament player who won the US PGA Championship in 1965. A Texan, Dave had all the broad humour of that state. He was very quick-witted. When viewing a canny old campaigner on the course who was getting away with murder, using all his guile to scrape a par here and the odd birdie there, he would say, 'Yes, he's a hard old dog to keep under the porch.'

When there was a David and Goliath situation he'd say, 'Well lookee here, the lamb jumped up and bit the butcher!'

Dave thought golf had become a 'lift and drop' game as the years went by. If someone was tearing up the course, out in 31 and putting for a birdie on the 10th (could he be thinking of one Tiger Woods?), he'd say, 'He's hotter than a bucket of red ants.'

For someone playing conservatively, sitting back watching his opponent make mistakes, Dave would say, 'Why dig for bait when you've got a boat full of fish!'

Barry Johnston:

Renton Laidlaw, for many years the anchor of the European Tour coverage on the Golf Channel, was the first European to receive the PGA of America's Lifetime Achievement Award in Journalism. One suspects that it was not awarded for the commentary when the Scotsman informed his viewers, 'Paul Azinger is wearing an all-black outfit: black jumper, blue trousers, white shoes and a pink tea-cosy hat!'

Robert Sommers:

In the early years of ABC golf telecasts, Chris Schenkel, then the network's leading sports announcer, teamed with Byron Nelson on golf commentary. Noting the players' long drives during one of the winter-tour tournaments, Schenkel led Nelson into explaining the reason for this phenomenon.

Obviously a little nervous, since this was one of his early exposures to announcing, Nelson responded by expounding, 'Chris, the boys are hitting the ball longer now because they're getting more distance!'

Alex Hay:

The technical criticisms do not worry the commentator too much, for viewers cannot be expected to know what goes on behind the scenes. What can hurt is when the person is attacked. In my own case, it is my accent that causes more critical correspondence, and all of it from Scotland.

The Scots think I am trying to be an Englishman; they do not realise that when you leave your country at the age of nineteen and live in another for almost twice that long, certain changes will take place in your pronunciation, and though the English think I am very Scottish, many Scots do not agree. One wrote to me and asked, 'Why don't you pronounce BURDIE and FURST correctly? If they were meant to be "birdie" and "first" they'd be spelt with I's and not U's!'

And he was serious; the rest of his letter is unprintable!

Tom Cox: *Bring Me the Head of Sergio Garcia!*

I don't wish to denigrate the higher plateaux of the golfing profession. I understand that in a sporting environment not without its history of blackballing, where you're rubbing shoulders with the same people week in and week out, there is little social sense in making a controversial statement about your contemporaries.

I also understand that the mindset that comes up with choice *bons mots* is not necessarily one that is able to roll forty-foot putts stone dead under pressure. All the same, would it be such a tragedy if *someone said something interesting in an interview sometime*? It wouldn't even have to be about golf. It could be about go-karting, or kettles, or iceberg lettuce.

During the periods I spent watching televised golf in 2006, I sometimes questioned my motives for turning pro. Maybe I did want to put my golfing ability to the ultimate test. But perhaps I really just wanted to put myself in a position where I could subvert the post-round interview custom of answering every question with one of – or a slight variation of one of – the following three statements:

(a) 'Well, you know, it's all just about making a few putts. And today I didn't make any putts.'

(b) 'Well, it's all just about hitting the greens. And today I didn't hit any greens.'

(c) 'We'll just see how it goes. I've just got to take every shot as it comes, and not really think about tomorrow.'

People think politicians do the ultimate line in interrogative stonewalling, but they have nothing on golfers. If you listen carefully, there's actually a great skill to it. It's as if, at some point on their road to stardom – possibly shortly after perfecting their standardised 'I'd like to thank the greenstaff for the condition of the course' amateur victory speeches – the whole lot of them have been sent to secret seminars with titles like 'The Use of the Phrase "Y'Know" as a Delaying Tactic', 'Appearing to Evaluate Your Disaster on the Back Nine When Really You're Just Spouting Hot Air That Could Apply to Any Round of Golf', and (a favourite of Colin Montgomerie's, this) 'The Merits of "As it Were": How it Can Make You Look Articulate, When You're Saying Something Quite Obvious and Dull'. Long were the hours I'd spent dreaming about bringing my own brand of answers to the mix:

'So, Tom . . . sixty-seven today. That puts you just three shots behind Paul Casey, tied with Woody Austin. Still hope for tomorrow, then? And I suppose it could have been better still had you not had that bit of bad luck in the Road Bunker?'

'Well, Julian, you could call it bad luck, but the truth is, I bollocksed it up! Totally my fault! Should have knocked it on the green, but I got distracted. The problem was that I'd sort of drifted off and started thinking about how much I wanted a packet of Monster Munch.'

'Er . . . right. Were you thinking about the roast beef or pickled onion flavour?'

'Oh, pickled onion, naturally.'

'Well . . . remarkable! So, a birdie barrage on Sunday?'

'I'm buggered if I know. Probably not, I suppose, if I keep swinging like something halfway between Lee Trevino and that mushroom-headed creature you get on Supermario Golf. Also, I'm not that pleased about being paired with Woody Austin. He looks like a right bad-tempered git. Did you see him beating the crap out of himself with his club that time he missed that two-footer? I'm just looking forward to the next interview with you, to be honest!'

Barry Johnston:

My father, Brian Johnston, the BBC cricket commentator, did not take up playing golf until he was in his early sixties. He was never very good but he used to play occasionally at the scenic Isle of Purbeck Golf Club in Dorset. His friend Jim Swanton once said his ambition was to be a Second World War golfer – out in 39, back in 45!

In 1987 Brian was a guest on the television chat show *Wogan*, which was transmitted 'live' on BBC1 early in the evenings, and he nearly had the programme taken off the air.

After the host, Terry Wogan, had interviewed Brian for a few minutes, they were joined by Wogan's second guest, the comedian Ronnie Corbett, and the conversation turned quickly to golf. Corbett had just told an amusing anecdote about Jimmy Tarbuck when Brian suddenly blurted out, 'Have we got time for Tarby's story?' Wogan looked a bit surprised but told him to carry on.

'This golfer used to go around with a little white poodle,' explained Brian, 'and when he did a good drive or a good putt the poodle got up on his hind legs and clapped with his front paws. So Tarby said to this chap, "What happens if you miss a putt or get in a bunker?" And this chap said, "Oh, he turns a lot of somersaults." Jimmy said, "How many?" And the chap said, "It depends how hard I kick him up the arse!"'

There was a roar of laughter from the audience and a look of stunned amazement on the faces of Ronnie Corbett and Terry Wogan.

'That's not mine, it's Tarbuck's!' Brian said hurriedly.

'That Tarbuck doesn't care what he says,' complained Wogan. 'He's shameless. That's why he works for the other side . . . as indeed you may do after this!'

Ronnie Corbett still could not believe what he had heard. 'Is that the first time that word has been said at this time in the evening?' he enquired nervously.

'What word?' tempted Wogan.

'A . . . ,' said Corbett, stopping himself just in time, 'the . . . the *bottom* word.'

'No, we normally don't go further than "bottie",' muttered Wogan, before moving swiftly on to the next subject!

Barry Johnston:

TV presenter Steve Rider hosted *Sportsnight* and *Grandstand* on BBC Television for more than twenty years before moving to ITV Sport in 2006. He has said that his favourite golf courses to work at are Turnberry and the Old Course at Sunningdale, where he once announced, 'The par here at Sunningdale is seventy and anything under that will be a score in the sixties!'

Peter Alliss:

Craig Stadler was battling his way up the 18th hole at the PGA Championship a few years ago. The humidity was very high and it looked as though someone had thrown a couple of buckets of water over him. Dave Marr said, 'Here comes Stadler, dressed by the dreaded sisters, Polly and Esther!'

At a tee shot on a par-three hole, the player hits, the television commentator says, 'Ah, that's a little heavy.' The camera follows the flight of the ball, which ends a few feet from the hole. Dave Marr's comment is, 'Yes, a little heavy, but perfect – just like Liz Taylor!'

Of Steve Pate, he of the volcanic temper, Dave judged he was 'meaner than a junk-yard dog'. After a particular conversation with a relatively well-known golf aficionado, Dave turned to me and said, 'How is it that old bores never die?'

Mrs Bobbitt, you will remember, was the lady who became so displeased with her husband that she cut off the most private of his private parts and threw it out of the car window. From then on, if someone hit a wild slice, Marr would say that 'he's hit a Bobbitt!'

When the great Fanny Sunesson first started to get vocal when caddying for Nick Faldo – 'no cameras please', 'stand still' – Dave said, tongue in cheek, 'You know, Fanny's beginning to sound just like a first wife!'

When someone looked particularly agitated, having just dropped four strokes in a row, Dave would say, 'Stick a fork in him – he's done.' In more recent times, if a precocious young player overshot a green by a considerable distance, the gag would be, 'I guess he just pumped too much air into his Reeboks.'

And he said of Bernhard Langer on a particularly sombre day, 'His sense of humour is no laughing matter!'

Barry Johnston:

Nick Faldo did not always seek the advice of his caddie, Fanny Sunesson, when he was lining up his putts. This led to a classic piece of golf commentary. The Scottish former Ryder Cup player Ken Brown was commentating on television when he startled viewers with the observation, 'Some weeks Nick likes to use Fanny, other weeks he prefers to do it by himself!'

Barry Johnston:

During the 1979 Walker Cup at Muirfield, American teenager Doug Clarke stunned the crowds with a record 8 and 7 rout of the veteran Scottish amateur, John Davies. At one point Clarke blessed himself before attempting a bunker shot, but he left the ball in the sand.

Peter Alliss chuckled, 'You can't trust anybody these days!'

Alex Hay:

In my second week working with the BBC, I was at Sunningdale for the Colgate Ladies, a marvellous tournament that attracted the top women players of the world. Our commentary box was set by the trees on the far corner of that beautiful downhill dogleg on the 17th hole. When I arrived, I was told that Peter Alliss was in America doing the United States PGA Championship and Harry Carpenter was in Canada doing the Commonwealth Games.

'This is it,' I thought. 'A senior man after only one week.'

It was in that week that I learned one of the first lessons in golf commentary. What I had not realised is that the commentators should not look out of the window, but must watch the television monitor in front of them. This is so that their commentary matches the pictures the viewers are seeing at home.

By the third day I had not yet learned this lesson and was commentating on the gorgeous Marlene Floyd, who was in the bunker on the far side of the 17th hole, right opposite the box.

I remember suggesting that she mustn't go for the green from the sand, for she was only one shot behind Nancy Lopez. She should play safely to the fairway then go for the green from there. This would keep her in contention. To hit the bunker face and leave the ball in the sand would be disastrous.

As though she heard me, Marlene took the sand wedge and played it out towards the commentary box, a perfect shot.

That would normally be when the director would tell you to 'stop talking' and take viewers to another hole and bring in Clive Clark out on the course. Instead, because everyone on his vast array of screens was walking, he ordered me to 'talk!'

In that moment, while you gather your senses, thinking, 'What shall I say?' the cameraman behind the 17th tee powered up his zoom lens and crashed in on that yellow mini-skirted bottom as it wiggled the fifty yards towards the ball; he waited for my next comment.

Had I been looking at my monitor I would have seen this, but I was not, I was looking out of the window.

'Henry Cotton,' – I had thought of a point of interest – 'isn't this the finest little hole on the course?'

'Yes indeed,' replied the great man, also looking out of the window, 'but they were all much tighter in my day . . . !'

Barry Johnston:

When Jimmy Demaret appeared as a guest on *The Tonight Show* with Johnny Carson in the 1960s, he offered to help Carson with his golf swing. Carson, who was a keen amateur golfer, swung a club and asked Demaret what he thought. The three-time Masters champion stepped aside to get a different view and asked the talk-show host to swing again. And then again. 'Tell you what, Johnny,' he said finally. 'If I were you, I'd lay off for a couple of weeks.'

He paused and then added, 'And then I'd quit!'

Richie Benaud:

Peter Alliss of the modern-day golf commentators is outstanding and is a master of the pause and build-up. He was responsible for one of the best pieces of sports television commentary I have ever heard. It was during the Dunhill Masters at Woburn in 1985 when Seve Ballesteros was playing the 18th, which is normally the first hole for club members. It was very late in the tournament and Seve had slightly pulled his tee shot to within a yard or two of the fence alongside the road. He had been saved from being out of bounds by the ball brushing a gorse bush but his stance was still going to be impeded by more gorse.

Seve gave it everything when he arrived down there. He took his stance then he changed it, then he put on his waterproofs and took them off, and all the time there was the camera behind him at ground level. Alliss, after telling the viewers what kind of shot Seve might be able to fashion from virtually nothing and reminding them that a birdie was essential, remained quiet. There was plenty going on for the viewers to see, which is what television is all about, but there are some commentators who would have been chatting away and describing what the viewers could see for themselves.

When Seve finally settled into the gorse again and wriggled around several times with a very pained expression on his face as his buttocks were scratched and torn, Alliss finally used just one sentence to add to the picture and the viewers' enjoyment.

'Ah yes,' he said, 'but how will he explain all that to his wife when he gets home?'

IN THE CLUBHOUSE

Barry Johnston:

Major John Bywaters was the secretary of the Professional Golfers Association in the late 1960s. He used to tell a story about his first day as a golf club secretary. After spending the morning in his office he went into the lounge and saw, leaning against the bar, a tall individual with a weather-beaten face, wearing brown corduroy trousers and enjoying a pint of bitter.

Anxious to make a good impression, he went over to introduce himself and said brightly, 'Good morning, sir. It's a lovely day.'

It was the lady captain!

Peter Alliss:

The most famous hole in golf? The 19th, of course, yet it has little if anything to do with the game. It's the

267

favoured place in the clubhouse for a drink and companionship. After the game is over, the conversation flows over an orange juice or whatever you fancy. For many, this part of the golfing day – especially if the golf has not prospered – may prove to be the most enjoyable. Here every man and woman becomes an expert – in their eyes at least!

The talk ranges freely. Few topics are actually banned, though perhaps politics should be treated with caution. There's one subject above all to be avoided. No one, absolutely no one, is interested in how you played your last round. You have to be Woods or Els in a crowded press tent to find an interested audience, and even they have long ago learned that their fellow players care not in the least. As the great Bobby Locke used to say in kindly tones, 'How did you play today, Master . . . but please start at the eighteenth!'

I learned this lesson myself many years ago. I was in the company of my father, Percy, the Whitcombe brothers and Abe Mitchell, the greatest player to fail to win the Open Championship. Into the clubhouse came a dejected young man, Bill Laidlaw, an assistant to Henry Cotton at Ashridge. He was a most promising player whose career never came to fruition only because he was killed in the war. Seeing his dejection, Abe Mitchell said, 'What's the matter, son?'

This was a mistake. Bill proceeded to go through his round stroke by horrid stroke. There was the opening

drive out of bounds, an iron shot ruled on the flag that kicked sharp right into a pot bunker, a four-putt where the hole had been set just at the top of a rise and the ball returned to Bill's feet rather too often. So the account went on, the minutes ticked away. But we heard him out.

When the tale of disaster came to an end, the generally kind Abe Mitchell leaned forward and said, 'Yes, it's a sad story, lad. But remember this, no one but you gives a bugger!'

Barry Johnston:

A golfer walked into the clubhouse bar with some astounding news. 'Hey!' he said to the assembled members. 'You know that chap who kicked his ball out of the rough in last month's Saturday Medal? He's just been sentenced to thirty years in prison for multiple counts of rape, grievous bodily harm and arson!'

There was a stunned silence.

The Greens Committee Chairman looked aghast. 'He kicked his ball out of the rough?' he said. 'Well, he's in for a shock if he thinks he's playing *here* again in the next decade!'

Tim Brooke-Taylor:
DICTIONARY OF GOLFING TERMS

Address That which a golfer fails to give when driving his ball through a plate-glass window overlooking the course.

Back door Any shot which takes a pirouette before entering the hole and which is normally claimed as intentional by a club player.

Birdie A hole that is completed in 1-under-par. Thus, in the case of a par-four hole, a birdie is obtained when a player holes out in three lucky shots as opposed to four lucky shots.

Blast General form of verbal address given after playing a sand shot.

Bolt a putt When a putt is struck so hard it causes structural damage to the hole as it sinks.

Borrow What a player generally does when asked to stand a round in the clubhouse.

Cut shot Name given to any badly sliced shot that accidentally leaves the ball in a half-decent lie.

Divot Form of sod removed from the course by inexperienced player, as opposed to the greenkeeper, who is another form of sod that many would wish to remove from the course.

Dogleg Hole that the rank amateur is compelled by unnatural forces beyond his control to play in a straight line, in contrast to straight holes that he is compelled to play as doglegs.

Dormie That point at which a losing player decides that it should not be the result that matters but rather the act of playing, and upon this basis suggests that all bets should be recalled and the game played out purely for fun.

Eagle A hole in which a player uses up his year's quota of fluke shots in one go.

Fairway That which a player playing six on a long hole is heard to answer when asked how far it is to the flag.

Gimme A putt claimed when the ball lies within thirty feet of the apron.

Grasscutter The golfing equivalent of an Exocet; takes on the properties of a two-hundred-foot putt.

Halved A hole is halved when both players discover they have cheated equally.

Hazard Anything at all within a quarter of a mile of the tee that impedes progress.

Lie That in which the club golfer can compete on equal terms with the professional.

Lost ball Mysterious ball that having been lost for fifteen minutes suddenly discovers itself on the lip of the green.

Press To attempt to hit a ball three times farther than one has ever hit a golf ball before.

Rough Area of grass that is considered an artificial obstruction from which a player can drop out.

Rub of the green That which is deemed ill luck when adversely affecting one's own ball, and unfair luck when profiting an opponent.

Shank That by which one may secure a hole in one on holes adjacent to the one you are at present playing.

Sky Any ball that would secure a hole in one were the hole to be on a plateau two hundred feet directly above one's head.

Stance The position in which one stands immediately before clubbing an innocent tee to death.

Tee That which a player blames for everything when he misses his drive on the first hole.

Windmill A swing in which a player attempts to demonstrate the workings of the piston aero engine.
Woods Where most players go in search of their balls.

Barry Johnston:

One of the most unusual shots in golf history took
place during the first round of the 1974 English Open
Amateur Stroke Play Championship at Moortown Golf
Club, near Leeds. Nigel Denham hit his second shot to
the 18th green with such reckless abandon that it soared
over the green, bounced up some steps and through an
open door into the clubhouse. There it ricocheted off a
wall before coming to rest under a table in the club bar.

The clubhouse at Moortown was in bounds so Denham
was advised that his ball was still in play, although one
of the members drinking at the bar queried, 'Are you
allowed to play this watering hole before the eighteenth?
There should be a two-pint penalty!'

Before he could enter the clubhouse, Denham had to
remove his golf shoes. Then, after moving the table away
from his ball, he noticed that he could see the flagstick
on the 18th green through a window. He opened the
window, and cheered on by the assembled drinkers at the
bar, he pitched the ball perfectly to within twelve feet of
the hole. Then he strolled happily out on to the green
and holed the putt for a sensational par-four.

A few weeks later the R&A ruled that Nigel Denham had improved his line of play and should have been given a two-stroke penalty for opening the window. However, after further discussions with the USGA, they allowed Denham's score to stand. It was agreed that, after all, windows are made to be opened!

Michael Green: The Art of Coarse Golf

My friend Askew's seven-year-old daughter was recently asked to write an essay in school on the subject of sport. This was the result:

> *I am going to write about golf. My Daddy plays golf with Uncle Mike. Uncle Mike is very old, as old as Daddy. Uncle Mike has to play golf with my Daddy because he has no children of his own to keep him amused. I do not like Uncle Mike. He is not as nice as my other uncle who comes to sleep when Daddy is away on business.*
>
> *Uncle Mike used to give me presents sometimes, but he has stopped since I was sick in the back of his car. When Daddy and Uncle Mike go to play golf they come back smelling all funny. Daddy says it is Flowers.*
>
> *One day Daddy took me to watch him play golf with Uncle Mike. Mummy made him do it as she had*

to have her hair done. Uncle Mike was not pleased and asked Daddy why he couldn't have left the brat at home, preferably in the kitchen with all the gas taps turned on.

When they got to the golf course they went into a little room in a big house and changed their clothes and then they came out and waited with a lot of other men while some others hit the ball. They were all old men too.

When a man hit a ball he said 'Shave off' and ran to one side to watch it hit the trees and all the others said, 'Ardluck, Charlie,' but secretly I think they were pleased.

When Uncle Mike came to hit the ball he spent a long time waving his big club, and then he lifted it ever so high in the air and dug up a piece of earth with it and he was not pleased because he had been naughty and all the men looked at each other and said, 'Oh dear, what a naughty man.'

And I said, 'Are you digging for worms, Uncle Mike?' and they all laughed and one of them patted my head and said I was a clever girl, but I do not think Uncle Mike was pleased.

After Daddy had had his go he went into a little wood and Uncle Mike went into another little wood to look for their balls. Daddy found his ball under a bush. I got it out for him and he built a little mound of earth and put it on it and then he hit it out of the wood and went to help Uncle Mike who was looking into a drain.

I said to Uncle Mike, 'Daddy just found his ball under a bush and I got it out for him,' and Daddy tried to put his hand over my mouth but Uncle Mike said I was a good girl and gave me a sweetie.

Just then some naughty men came up and told Uncle Mike that if he had lost his ball he should let them have their little go, but Uncle Mike was rude.

Then Uncle Mike found his ball and he hit it into the drain again and we had to wait while a lot of other men had their go.

Daddy did not go into the wood again but he took ever such a little club and he went to play in a sand-pit like we have in the school playground only much bigger. Daddy played a lovely game throwing sand all over everywhere so I went into another sandpit next door and built a beautiful sandcastle with a real moat.

When I showed it to Daddy he went very red and said, 'Good God, look what the child's done,' and he and Uncle Mike went down on their hands and knees and flattened out my castle. While they were doing it a man came along on a sort of mowing machine and he said they ought to be ashamed of themselves and he would report them to the secretary, and Uncle Mike said that word again.

After that Daddy and Uncle Mike went to play on a little piece of flat ground with a lot of sand-pits round it and a big stick in the middle and Daddy let me hold the stick. It was in a nasty little hole full of water. So when Uncle Mike hit his ball I stopped it from rolling into the nasty hole and Uncle Mike threw his club at Daddy and it hit him on the knee. Daddy said, 'You can't blame me for what the child does,' and Uncle Mike said the only consolation was that I was as happy as if I was in my right senses.

Then we saw two lady golfers, and they were very old, as old as Mummy, and Uncle Mike said something to Daddy and they went away and whispered and came back laughing.

Then we came to a huge river and Daddy and Uncle Mike tried to see who could get most balls into it and my Daddy won because he hit the river more times, but he did not look pleased. Uncle Mike said would I like to go and look in the river for the balls, preferably in the deepest part, but I did not go.

Then they went to play on a bit with a stick in the middle again. Daddy took out his teeny-weeny club, the one he uses to practise with in the living-room. He stood on the grass near the long stick, and he looked hard at the ball and hard at the long stick and then he stood on one leg and then he started to breathe very heavily and then he asked Uncle Mike to stop blinking as the noise of his eyelids upset him.

Well, while Daddy was standing still and breathing hard I saw a squirrel and I whispered it to Uncle Mike, and he said, 'Go and tell Daddy now.' As Daddy was swinging his teeny-weeny club I ran up and shouted, 'Daddy, Daddy, Daddy, I've just seen a squirrel,' and he jumped and he hit the ball ever so hard, much harder than he hits it even with that big club with the lump on the end, and the ball went away into a sandpit.

Then Daddy went all sort of pale and trembly, like Diana Bradshaw when she was sick in the playground, and he kept twitching and muttering, and then he said, 'May God forgive me, but I want to kill my own daughter.'

Uncle Mike said would I pull his little truck for him as that might keep me quiet, and he let me pull the truck and I found it ever so easy and I ran round and round one of the long sticks just like a racetrack. But two nasty men came along and shouted at me and Uncle Mike took his little truck away from me and said if I had any more brains I would be half-witted.

Then we got back to where they started and we went into the big house and Daddy gave me a lemonade and Uncle Mike gave me sixpence and I put it

*into a big machine with coloured lights all over it,
and I pressed a handle and a lot of sixpences came
out of the bottom. Uncle Mike made a noise as if he
was going to be ill and said it was the irony of life
and now he had tasted the very dregs.*

*I shall not play golf when I grow up as it is a
stupid, silly game. I told Mummy so when she was
bathing me and she said I was right but men played it
because they were silly, stupid people and Uncle Mike
was the silliest and stupidest of them all.*

Angela Askew (Form IV)

There is a note on the end of the manuscript in the teacher's handwriting stating, 'There is no need to try and spell out the exact words used by your Daddy and his friend.'

ACKNOWLEDGEMENTS

I would like to thank all the authors and publishers who have given their permission for extracts from their work to be reproduced in this book. In particular I would like to express my special thanks to John Ireland for another wonderful set of illustrations. I am also most grateful to everyone at Hodder & Stoughton for their help and advice, especially Rupert Lancaster, Roddy Bloomfield, Laura Macaulay and Loreen Brown. Last, but definitely not least, many thanks to my copy-editor, Marion Paull, for her diligent work correcting the manuscript.

Extracts from the following books have been reproduced by kind permission of their publishers:

Alliss, Peter: *My Life* (Hodder & Stoughton, 2004); Alliss, Peter: *Golf: The Cure For a Grumpy Old Man* (Hodder & Stoughton, 2008); Benaud, Richie: *My Spin on Cricket* (Hodder & Stoughton, 2005); Brooke-Taylor,

Tim: *Tim Brooke-Taylor's Golf Bag* (Stanley Paul/ Arrow, The Random House Group, 1988); Campbell, Patrick: *Patrick Campbell's Golfing Book* (Blond & Briggs, The Random House Group, 1972); Corbett, Ronnie: *High Hopes: My Autobiography* (Ebury Press, The Random House Group, 2000); Cox, Tom: *Bring Me the Head of Sergio Garcia!* (Yellow Jersey Press, The Random House Group, 2008); Daly, John: *My Life In and Out of the Rough* (HarperCollins Publishers, 2006); Donegan, Lawrence: *Quiet Please* (Yellow Jersey Press, The Random House Group, 2004); Faldo, Nick: *Life Swings* (Headline, 2004); Forsyth, Bruce: *Bruce: The Autobiography* (Sidgwick & Jackson, Pan Macmillan, 2001); Hay, Alex: *Ripening Hay* (Partridge Press, The Random House Group, 1989); Jacklin, Tony: *Jacklin: My Autobiography* (Simon & Schuster, 2006); Johnston, Barry: *Johnners: The Life of Brian* (Hodder & Stoughton, 2003); Keating, Frank: *Classic Moments From a Century of Sport* (Robson Books, Anova Books Company, 1997); Lyle, Sandy: *To The Fairway Born* (Headline, 2006); O'Connor, Tom: *From the Wood to the Tees* (Robson Books, Anova Books Company, 1992); Parkinson, Michael: *On Golf* (Hodder & Stoughton, 1999); Rice, Jonathan: *Classic After-Dinner Sports Tales* (HarperCollins Publishers, 2004); Sommers, Robert: *Golf Anecdotes* (Oxford University Press, 1995); Torrance, Sam: *Sam* (BBC Books, The Random House

Group, 2003); Wooldridge, Ian: *Searching for Heroes* (Hodder & Stoughton, 2007); Woosnam, Ian: *Woosie: My Autobiography* (HarperCollins Publishers, 2002).

The extract by Martin Johnson from the *Sunday Times* is © *The Times* and 31.05.2009/nisyndication.com; extracts by Martin Johnson from the *Daily Telegraph* are © Telegraph Media Group Ltd, 2009.

'Seaside Golf' from *Collected Poems* by John Betjeman (© 1955–2001) is reproduced by permission of John Murray (Publishers); extracts from *The Book of Golf Disasters* by Peter Dobereiner (© Peter Dobereiner, 1983) and *Dobereiner on Golf* by Peter Dobereiner (© Peter Dobereiner, 1998) are reprinted by permission of A.M. Heath & Co Ltd; extracts from *The Art of Coarse Golf* by Michael Green (© Michael Green, 1971) are reproduced by permission of Sheil Land Associates Ltd; extracts from *The Heart of a Goof, Ordeal by Golf, The Salvation of George Mackintosh* and *Tangled Hearts* appearing in *The Golf Omnibus* by P.G. Wodehouse (Hutchinson) are reprinted by permission of The Random House Group Ltd.

Among other books consulted, particular use was made of the following: *The Wit & Wisdom of Golf* by Nick Holt; *The New Quotable Golfer* by Robert McCord; *Great Golf Quotes* by Michael McDonnell. Many excellent golf websites were also a valuable source of information, including: golf.com; golfdigest.com;

golfjokes.com; masters.com; opengolf.com; pgatour. com; standrews.com; usopen.com; and many others. While every effort has been made to trace all copyright holders, the publishers would be pleased to hear from any not here acknowledged.

INDEX

285

Index

Index